The Ninja Creami Deluxe Cookbook 2024

Savor Frozen Bliss: Easy, Healthy Recipes for Summer! Indulge in Homemade Ice Cream, Sorbets, Creamiccino, Milkshakes, Italian ice, Gelato, and More Cool Desserts

Jared Rodgers

CONTENTS

INTRODUCTION

Welcome to the wonderful world of frozen delights! Prepare for a delicious adventure with this cookbook, where creativity and indulgence blend together in a delightful way. Whether you're a seasoned ice cream lover or just starting to explore the world of frozen desserts, prepare yourself for a taste sensation that surpasses anything you can buy at the store.

After experiencing the delightful regular Ninja CREAMi, it's hard to resist the allure of the deluxe edition, which is only available to a privileged few. Picture this: a modern appliance with 11 programs, each offering a distinct frozen experience. The Ninja CREAMi Deluxe is the perfect tool for creating a variety of delicious frozen treats, from creamy gelatos to refreshing sorbets, traditional ice creams to innovative creamiccinos, refreshing milkshakes to nutritious smoothie bowls. Get ready to indulge!

Inside this book, you'll find a collection of carefully selected recipes that are not only delicious but also packed with nutritional benefits. Each recipe is guaranteed to bring you joy. This cookbook offers a wide range of delicious frozen treats, an adventure that caters to all taste buds.

Experience the excitement as you dive into the recipes, get creative with flavors, and fully embrace the pure joy of creating your own one-of-a-kind frozen treats.

Unveiling the Potential of Your Ninja Creami Deluxe

Congrats on acquiring the Ninja Creami Deluxe! This revolutionary appliance offers a whole new level of frozen treats. It effortlessly turns ordinary ingredients into delectable ice cream, gelato, sorbet, milkshakes, and more in just minutes. However, the Creami Deluxe goes beyond simply producing basic treats; it serves as a platform for limitless creativity and personalization.

Here's a glimpse into the exciting possibilities that await you:

- **Effortless Frozen Treats:** Say goodbye to the tedious process of churning and waiting for hours. The Creami Deluxe, with its unique freezing technology, swiftly creates delicious frozen treats. There is no need to pre-freeze bowls or follow complicated steps—simply add your ingredients and let the machine work its magic. It's a kitchen companion that takes the stress out of dessert making.

- **Beyond the Basics:** The Creami Deluxe offers a wide range of options beyond the traditional flavors of vanilla and chocolate. You can add flavor to your ice cream by incorporating fresh fruits, spices, or even your favorite candy mix-ins. Try out different bases and make your own delicious creations—from healthy yogurt parfaits to indulgent gelato made with rich cream.

- **Portion Control Perfection:** Looking for a delicious ice cream treat that's perfect for one? Not a problem! The Creami Deluxe lets you make single servings, so you won't be tempted to overindulge from a big container. This is great for managing portion sizes or experimenting with different flavors without excess leftovers.

- **Dietary Freedom:** The Creami Deluxe empowers you to customize your frozen treats to suit your specific dietary requirements. Opt for low-fat yogurt to make a lighter choice, experiment with plant-based milks to create vegan ice cream, or try out sugar-free alternatives. With the Creami Deluxe, you can indulge in your favorite treats guilt-free.

- **Endless Customization:** The Creami Deluxe is not just for frozen desserts. It's a gateway to a world of culinary creativity. Explore beyond traditional ice cream and discover new options like savory frozen yogurt dips, nutritious smoothie bowls, or refreshing frozen cocktails (for adults only!).

The possibilities are as limitless as your imagination. This is just the beginning of your frozen adventure with the Ninja Creami Deluxe. Get ready to unleash your creativity, explore new flavor combinations, and discover the endless potential this innovative appliance has to offer!

A Guide to Creami Parts and Functions

It's essential to have a good grasp of the various components and their functions to fully utilize the capabilities of your Ninja Creami Deluxe. Let's dive into the key components and see how they come together to make your beloved frozen treats:

Base Unit:

- The heart of the machine, houses the powerful motor and intuitive control panel.

- The control panel features buttons for selecting pre-programmed cycles (like Ice Cream or Sorbet), adjusting settings (like mixing time), and initiating the freezing process.

Creami Pint Container:

- This double-walled, insulated container is where the magic happens! It holds your frozen ingredients and securely attaches to the base unit for processing.

- Thanks to the lid that prevents leaks, you can easily store your leftover creations in the freezer for later enjoyment.

Creami Spindles:

- These are the interchangeable heroes of the Creami Deluxe. Each spindle is specifically designed to create a different frozen texture.

- The Ice Cream Spindle breaks down frozen ingredients into a smooth, creamy consistency for classic ice cream and gelato.

- The Sorbet Spindle incorporates more air for a lighter, icy texture that is perfect for sorbets and frozen yogurt.

- The Milkshake Spindle is designed to handle thicker ingredients like fruits and mix-ins, resulting in a spoon-thick milkshake consistency. (Note: Additional spindles may be available depending on your specific Creami Deluxe model)

Mixing Paddle (Optional):

- This paddle attachment is ideal for thicker creations like smoothie bowls or frozen yogurt parfaits.

- It attaches to the base unit and spins to combine ingredients without incorporating air, resulting in a denser consistency.

Tamper (Optional):

- This convenient tool ensures that ingredients in the Creami Pint Container are evenly processed by applying gentle pressure.

- It's particularly useful for thicker ingredients or when filling the container.

By understanding the function of each part and how they work together, you'll be well on your way to mastering your Ninja Creami Deluxe and creating endless frozen masterpieces!

The Different Functions of the Ninja Creami Deluxe

The Ninja Creami Deluxe boasts 11 pre-programmed settings designed to transform your frozen treat dreams into reality. Here's a breakdown of what each function offers:

- **Ice Cream:** This setting is your go-to for creating classic, scoopable ice cream with a smooth, dense texture.

- **Lite Ice Cream:** Perfect for those seeking a lighter option, this cycle reduces the amount of air incorporated into the ice cream, resulting in a lower-calorie frozen treat.

- **Sorbet:** Calling all fruit lovers! This function creates refreshing sorbets with a light, icy texture ideal for showcasing vibrant fruit flavors.

- **Gelato:** For a denser and richer frozen treat than ice cream, the gelato setting emulates the luxurious texture of authentic Italian gelato.

- **Frozen Yogurt:** This program is perfect for creating healthy frozen yogurt treats using your favorite yogurts and mix-ins.

- **Creamiccino™:** This unique setting is designed for creating frothy, coffee-based frozen drinks like creamy cappuccinos or decadent frappes. (Note: Creamiccino™ is a trademarked term by Ninja)

- **Frozen Drink:** This versatile setting allows you to whip up refreshing frozen cocktails (for adults only!), smoothie blends, or icy slushies.

- **Slushi:** Hot day? Beat the heat with this setting, which creates cool and flavorful slushies in seconds and is perfect for satisfying summer cravings.

- **Italian Ice:** Enjoy the taste of classic Italian Ice with this function, which results in a denser and chewier frozen treat than sorbet.

- **Milkshake:** Craving a thick and creamy milkshake? This setting is designed to incorporate mix-ins like fruits, cookies, or chocolate chips for a delightful milkshake experience.

- **Mix-In:** This unique feature enables you to incorporate your preferred mix-ins into a pre-made frozen base, resulting in a wide range of flavor combinations while maintaining the overall texture.

Furthermore, the Ninja Creami Deluxe provides a Re-Spin function that lets you quickly process your frozen treat after it's dispensed, resulting in a smoother texture.

With this array of functions, the Ninja Creami Deluxe empowers you to create a wide variety of frozen treats, from classic favorites to your own unique concoctions. So grab your favorite ingredients, unleash your creativity, and explore the endless possibilities!

Cleaning & Maintaining Your Ninja Creami Deluxe
Regular Cleaning Steps:

1. **Unplug the Unit**: Before cleaning, always unplug your Ninja Creami Deluxe to ensure safety.

2. **Disassemble the Parts**:
   - Remove the lid, mixing paddle, and any other detachable components.
   - Rinse them under warm water to remove any residue.

3. **Wipe the Base Unit**:
   - Use a damp cloth to wipe the base unit. Avoid submerging it in water.

4. **Clean the Mixing Paddle and Lid**:
   - Wash the mixing paddle and lid with warm, soapy water.
   - Rinse thoroughly and let them air dry.

5. **Clean the Freezer Bowl**:

- Remove the freezer bowl from the unit.

- Wash it with mild soap and warm water.

- Dry completely before reassembling.

6. **Deep Cleaning (Monthly)**:

   - Mix equal parts of water and white vinegar.

   - Run the mixture through the machine to clean the internal components.

   - Rinse thoroughly afterward.

Maintenance Tips:

- **Avoid Abrasive Cleaners**: Do not use abrasive materials or harsh chemicals on any part of the Ninja Creami Deluxe.

- **Inspect Seals and Gaskets**: Regularly check the seals and gaskets for wear or damage. Replace if necessary.

- **Store Properly**: When not in use, store the Ninja Creami Deluxe with the lid on to prevent dust and debris from entering.

Remember, a well-maintained Ninja Creami Deluxe ensures delicious frozen treats every time!

Chapter 1: Ice Creams

Honey Lavender Ice Cream

Time to Prepare: 25 minutes
Ninja Creami Time: 5 minutes
Number of Servings: 4

Ingredients

- 1 cup of heavy cream
- 1 cup of whole milk
- 1/2 cup of honey
- 1/4 cup of granulated sugar
- 2 tablespoons dried culinary lavender
- 1 teaspoon of vanilla extract

Instructions List:

1. In a saucepan over medium heat, combine the heavy cream, whole milk, honey, granulated sugar, and dried lavender. Stir until the sugar is dissolved and the mixture is heated through, about 5-7 minutes. Do not boil.

2. Remove from heat and let the mixture steep for 15 minutes to infuse the lavender flavor.

3. Strain the mixture through a fine mesh sieve to remove the lavender buds.

4. Stir in the vanilla extract.

5. Pour the mixture into the Ninja Creami Deluxe pint container and secure the lid.

6. Place the container in the freezer and freeze for 24 hours.

7. After freezing, remove the container from the freezer and place it into the Ninja Creami Deluxe machine.

8. Select the "Ice Cream" function and start the machine.

9. Once the cycle is complete, remove the pint container from the machine and serve immediately.

Nutritional Information (per serving)

- Calories: 320
- Protein: 4g
- Total Fats: 18g
- Fiber: 0g
- Carbohydrates: 38g

Dark Chocolate Cherry Ice Cream

Time to Prepare: 20 minutes
Ninja Creami Time: 5 minutes
Number of Servings: 4

Ingredients

- 1 cup of heavy cream
- 1 cup of whole milk
- 3/4 cup granulated sugar
- 1/2 cup of dark chocolate, melted
- 1/2 cup of chopped cherries (fresh or frozen, pitted)
- 1 teaspoon of vanilla extract

Instructions List:

1. In a medium bowl, whisk together the heavy cream, whole milk, granulated sugar, melted dark chocolate, and vanilla extract until the sugar is dissolved and the mixture is smooth.
2. Fold in the chopped cherries.
3. Pour the mixture into the Ninja Creami Deluxe pint container and secure the lid.
4. Place the container in the freezer and freeze for 24 hours.
5. After freezing, remove the container from the freezer and place it into the Ninja Creami Deluxe machine.
6. Select the "Ice Cream" function and start the machine.
7. Once the cycle is complete, remove the pint container from the machine and serve immediately.

Nutritional Information (per serving)

- Calories: 350
- Protein: 5g
- Total Fats: 22g
- Fiber: 2g
- Carbohydrates: 36g

Earl Grey Tea Ice Cream

Time to Prepare: 30 minutes
Ninja Creami Time: 5 minutes
Number of Servings: 4

Ingredients

- 1 cup of heavy cream
- 1 cup of whole milk
- 3/4 cup granulated sugar
- 3 Earl Grey tea bags
- 1 teaspoon of vanilla extract

Instructions List:

1. In a saucepan over medium heat, combine the heavy cream and whole milk. Heat until just simmering, then remove from heat.

2. Add the Earl Grey tea bags to the saucepan and steep for 10 minutes. Remove the tea bags, squeezing out any liquid.

3. Stir in the granulated sugar until dissolved. Let the mixture cool to room temperature.

4. Stir in the vanilla extract.

5. Pour the mixture into the Ninja Creami Deluxe pint container and secure the lid.

6. Place the container in the freezer and freeze for 24 hours.

7. After freezing, remove the container from the freezer and place it into the Ninja Creami Deluxe machine.

8. Select the "Ice Cream" function and start the machine.

9. Once the cycle is complete, remove the pint container from the machine and serve immediately.

Nutritional Information (per serving)

- Calories: 310

- Protein: 4g

- Total Fats: 18g

- Fiber: 0g

- Carbohydrates: 35g

Brown Butter Pecan Ice Cream

Time to Prepare: 25 minutes
Ninja Creami Time: 5 minutes
Number of Servings: 4

Ingredients

- 1 cup of heavy cream

- 1 cup of whole milk

- 3/4 cup granulated sugar

- 1/2 cup of unsalted butter

- 1 teaspoon of vanilla extract

- 1 cup of chopped pecans

Instructions List:

1. In a saucepan over medium heat, melt the unsalted butter until it becomes golden brown and develops a nutty aroma, about 5-7 minutes. Remove from heat and let cool slightly.

2. In a medium bowl, whisk together the heavy cream, whole milk, granulated sugar, and vanilla extract until the sugar is dissolved.

3. Slowly whisk in the browned butter until fully mixed.

4. Pour the mixture into the Ninja Creami Deluxe pint container and secure the lid.

5. Place the container in the freezer and freeze for 24 hours.

6. After freezing, remove the container from the freezer and place it into the Ninja Creami Deluxe machine.

7. Select the "Ice Cream" function and start the machine.

8. Once the cycle is complete, remove the pint container from the machine.

9. Create a well in the center of the ice cream and add the chopped pecans.

10. Place the pint container back into the Ninja Creami Deluxe and select the "Mix-in" function.

11. Once the mix-in cycle is complete, remove the container and serve immediately.

Nutritional Information (per serving)

- Calories: 400

- Protein: 4g

- Total Fats: 30g

- Fiber: 1g

- Carbohydrates: 32g

Thai Tea Ice Cream

Time to Prepare: 30 minutes
Ninja Creami Time: 5 minutes
Number of Servings: 4

Ingredients

- 1 cup of heavy cream

- 1 cup of whole milk

- 3/4 cup granulated sugar

- 4 Thai tea bags

- 1 teaspoon of vanilla extract

Instructions List:

1. In a saucepan over medium heat, combine the heavy cream and whole milk. Heat until just simmering, then remove from heat.

2. Add the Thai tea bags to the saucepan and steep for 10 minutes. Remove the tea bags, squeezing out any liquid.

3. Stir in the granulated sugar until dissolved. Let the mixture cool to room temperature.

4. Stir in the vanilla extract.

5. Pour the mixture into the Ninja Creami Deluxe pint container and secure the lid.

6. Place the container in the freezer and freeze for 24 hours.

7. After freezing, remove the container from the freezer and place it into the Ninja Creami Deluxe machine.

8. Select the "Ice Cream" function and start the machine.

9. Once the cycle is complete, remove the pint container from the machine and serve immediately.

Nutritional Information (per serving)

- Calories: 320

- Protein: 4g

- Total Fats: 18g

- Fiber: 0g

- Carbohydrates: 37g

Saffron Pistachio Ice Cream

Time to Prepare: 30 minutes
Ninja Creami Time: 5 minutes
Number of Servings: 4

Ingredients

- 1 cup of heavy cream

- 1 cup of whole milk

- 3/4 cup granulated sugar

- 1 teaspoon of saffron threads

- 1 teaspoon of vanilla extract

- 1/2 cup of chopped pistachios

Instructions List:

1. In a small bowl, steep saffron threads in 2 tablespoons of warm milk for 10 minutes.

2. In a medium bowl, whisk together the heavy cream, whole milk, granulated sugar, and saffron-infused milk until the sugar is dissolved.

3. Stir in the vanilla extract.

4. Pour the mixture into the Ninja Creami Deluxe pint container and secure the lid.

5. Place the container in the freezer and freeze for 24 hours.

6. After freezing, remove the container from the freezer and place it into the Ninja Creami Deluxe machine.

7. Select the "Ice Cream" function and start the machine.

8. Once the cycle is complete, remove the pint container from the machine.

9. Create a well in the center of the ice cream and add the chopped pistachios.

10. Place the pint container back into the Ninja Creami Deluxe and select the "Mix-in" function.

11. Once the mix-in cycle is complete, remove the container and serve immediately.

Nutritional Information (per serving)

- Calories: 350

- Protein: 6g

- Total Fats: 23g

- Fiber: 2g

- Carbohydrates: 30g

Roasted Banana Cinnamon Ice Cream

Time to Prepare: 10 minutes (plus freezing time) **Ninja Creami Time:** 60 seconds **Servings:** 2-3

Ingredients:

- 2 ripe bananas, peeled and sliced

- 1 tablespoon of melted coconut oil

- 1 tablespoon of brown sugar

- 1/2 teaspoon of ground cinnamon

- 1/4 cup of unsweetened almond milk

- 1/2 teaspoon of vanilla extract

Instructions List:

1. Preheat oven to 400°F (200°C). In a small bowl, toss banana slices with melted coconut oil, brown sugar, and cinnamon. Spread evenly on a baking sheet lined with parchment paper.

2. Bake for 15-20 minutes, or until bananas are softened and lightly golden brown.

3. Transfer roasted bananas to a blender or food processor. Add almond milk and vanilla extract. Blend until smooth and creamy.

4. Pour mixture into a Ninja Creami Pint Container and freeze for a minimum of 8 hours, or overnight.

5. Attach the Ice Cream Spindle to the Ninja Creami Deluxe base unit. Place frozen banana mixture in the container and secure the lid.

6. Select the "Ice Cream" function and press "Start." Enjoy your homemade Roasted Banana Cinnamon Ice Cream immediately after bringing it out.

Nutritional Information (per serving):

- Calories: 250

- Protein: 2g

- Total Fats: 15g

- Fiber: 2g

- Carbohydrates: 30g

Lemon Blueberry Cheesecake Ice Cream

Time to Prepare: 15 minutes (plus freezing time) **Ninja Creami Time:** 60 seconds **Servings:** 4-5

Ingredients:

- 8 ounces softened cream cheese

- 1/4 cup of granulated sugar

- 1/4 cup of honey

- 1/2 teaspoon of lemon zest

- 1/4 cup of lemon juice

- 1/2 cup of plain Greek yogurt

- 1/2 cup of milk

- 1 teaspoon of vanilla extract

- 1 cup of fresh or frozen blueberries

Instructions List:

1. In a large bowl, cream together softened cream cheese, sugar, and honey until light and fluffy. Beat in lemon zest and juice until well mixed.

2. In a separate bowl, whisk together Greek yogurt, milk, and vanilla extract.

3. Fold the yogurt mixture into the cream cheese mixture until just mixed. Gently fold in blueberries, reserving a handful for garnish.

4. Pour the mixture into a Ninja Creami Pint Container and freeze for a minimum of 8 hours, or overnight.

5. Attach the Ice Cream Spindle to the Ninja Creami Deluxe base unit. Place frozen mixture in the container and secure the lid.

6. Select the "Ice Cream" function and press "Start." After processing, swirl in the reserved blueberries with a spoon.

7. Enjoy your Lemon Blueberry Cheesecake Ice Cream immediately after bringing it out.

Nutritional Information (per serving):

- Calories: 300

- Protein: 5g

- Total Fats: 18g

- Fiber: 2g

- Carbohydrates: 30g

Spicy Mexican Chocolate Ice Cream

Time to Prepare: 10 minutes (plus freezing time) **Ninja Creami Time:** 60 seconds **Servings:** 2-3

Ingredients:

- 1 cup of unsweetened almond milk (or whole milk for a richer version)

- 1/2 cup of heavy cream

- 1/4 cup of unsweetened cocoa powder

- 1/4 cup of granulated sugar

- 1/4 teaspoon of ground cinnamon

- 1/8 teaspoon cayenne pepper (adjust to your spice preference)

- 1/2 teaspoon of vanilla extract

- Pinch of salt

Instructions List:

1. In a saucepan, whisk together almond milk, heavy cream, cocoa powder, sugar, cinnamon, cayenne pepper, and salt. Heat over medium heat, stirring constantly, until sugar dissolves and mixture simmers gently. Do not boil.

2. Remove from heat and stir in vanilla extract. Let cool completely, then refrigerate for at least 2 hours, or until well chilled.

3. Pour the chilled chocolate mixture into a Ninja Creami Pint Container and freeze for a minimum of 8 hours, or overnight.

4. Attach the Ice Cream Spindle to the Ninja Creami Deluxe base unit. Place frozen mixture in the container and secure the lid.

5. Select the "Ice Cream" function and press "Start." Enjoy your Spicy Mexican Chocolate Ice Cream immediately after bringing it out.

Nutritional Information (per serving, using almond milk):

- Calories: 350

- Protein: 4g

- Total Fats: 25g

- Fiber: 1g

- Carbohydrates: 20g

Toasted Coconut Almond Ice Cream

Time to Prepare: 10 minutes (plus freezing time) **Ninja Creami Time:** 60 seconds **Servings:** 2-3

Ingredients:

- 1 cup of full-fat coconut milk

- 1/2 cup of unsweetened almond milk

- 1/4 cup of chopped toasted almonds

- 1/4 cup of shredded unsweetened coconut, toasted (reserve some for garnish)

- 1/4 cup of maple syrup

- 1/2 teaspoon of vanilla extract

- Pinch of salt

Instructions List:

1. In a small skillet, toast the chopped almonds over medium heat until fragrant and lightly golden brown, stirring frequently. Watch closely to avoid burning. Transfer to a plate to cool.

2. In a blender, combine coconut milk, almond milk, toasted almonds, toasted coconut (except reserved garnish), maple syrup, vanilla extract, and salt. Blend until smooth and creamy.

3. Pour the mixture into a Ninja Creami Pint Container and freeze for a minimum of 8 hours, or overnight.

4. Attach the Ice Cream Spindle to the Ninja Creami Deluxe base unit. Place frozen mixture in the container and secure the lid.

5. Select the "Ice Cream" function and press "Start." After processing, sprinkle with reserved toasted coconut for garnish (optional).

6. Enjoy your Toasted Coconut Almond Ice Cream immediately after bringing it out.

Nutritional Information (per serving):

- Calories: 350

- Protein: 4g

- Total Fats: 20g

- Fiber: 2g

- Carbohydrates: 30g

Peach Bourbon Ice Cream

Time to Prepare: 15 minutes (plus freezing time) **Ninja Creami Time:** 60 seconds **Servings:** 4-5

Ingredients:

- 2 ripe peaches, peeled and pitted, diced

- 1/4 cup of granulated sugar

- 1 tablespoon of cornstarch

- 1/4 cup of water

- 1 tablespoon of bourbon (optional, for adults only)

- 1 cup of heavy cream

- 1/2 cup of whole milk

- 1/2 teaspoon of vanilla extract

- Pinch of salt

Instructions List:

1. In a saucepan, combine diced peaches, sugar, and cornstarch. Stir over medium heat until sugar dissolves and mixture thickens slightly, about 5 minutes. Remove from heat and stir in water and bourbon (if using). Let cool completely.

2. In a separate bowl, whisk together heavy cream, milk, vanilla extract, and salt.

3. Combine the cooled peach mixture with the cream mixture. Pour the mixed mixture into a Ninja Creami Pint Container and freeze for a minimum of 8 hours, or overnight.

4. Attach the Ice Cream Spindle to the Ninja Creami Deluxe base unit. Place frozen mixture in the container and secure the lid.

5. Select the "Ice Cream" function and press "Start." Enjoy your Peach Bourbon Ice Cream immediately after bringing it out.

Nutritional Information (per serving, without bourbon):

- Calories: 300
- Protein: 3g
- Total Fats: 20g
- Fiber: 1g (from peaches)
- Carbohydrates: 30g

Raspberry White Chocolate Ice Cream

Time to Prepare: 10 minutes (plus freezing time) **Ninja Creami Time:** 60 seconds **Servings:** 2-3

Ingredients:

- 1 cup of fresh or frozen raspberries
- 1/4 cup of granulated sugar
- 1/2 cup of unsweetened almond milk (or whole milk for a richer version)
- 1/2 cup of heavy cream
- 8 ounces white chocolate chips
- 1/2 teaspoon of vanilla extract
- Pinch of salt

Instructions List:

1. In a blender, combine raspberries and sugar. Blend until smooth, then strain mixture through a fine-mesh sieve to remove seeds.
2. In a saucepan, heat almond milk and cream over medium heat until simmering gently. Do not boil. Remove from heat and stir in white chocolate chips until melted and smooth.
3. Let the mixture cool slightly, then stir in the strained raspberry puree, vanilla extract, and salt.
4. Pour the mixture into a Ninja Creami Pint Container and freeze for a minimum of 8 hours, or overnight.
5. Attach the Ice Cream Spindle to the Ninja Creami Deluxe base unit. Place frozen mixture in the container and secure the lid.
6. Select the "Ice Cream" function and press "Start." Enjoy your Raspberry White Chocolate Ice Cream immediately after bringing it out.

Nutritional Information (per serving, using almond milk):

- Calories: 400
- Protein: 4g
- Total Fats: 25g
- Fiber: 1g (from raspberries)
- Carbohydrates: 35g

Chapter 2: Ice Cream Mix-ins

Brownie Bits and Caramel Swirl

Time to Prepare: 25 minutes
Ninja Creami Time: 5 minutes
Number of Servings: 4

Ingredients

- 1 cup of heavy cream

- 1 cup of whole milk

- 3/4 cup granulated sugar

- 1 teaspoon of vanilla extract

- 1 cup of brownie bits (pre-cooked and chopped)

- 1/2 cup of caramel sauce

Instructions List:

1. In a medium bowl, whisk together the heavy cream, whole milk, granulated sugar, and vanilla extract until the sugar is dissolved.

2. Pour the mixture into the Ninja Creami Deluxe pint container and secure the lid.

3. Place the container in the freezer and freeze for 24 hours.

4. After freezing, remove the container from the freezer and place it into the Ninja Creami Deluxe machine.

5. Select the "Ice Cream" function and start the machine.

6. Once the cycle is complete, remove the pint container from the machine.

7. Create a well in the center of the ice cream and add the brownie bits and caramel sauce.

8. Place the pint container back into the Ninja Creami Deluxe and select the "Mix-in" function.

9. Once the mix-in cycle is complete, remove the container and serve immediately.

Nutritional Information (per serving)

- Calories: 420

- Protein: 5g

- Total Fats: 24g

- Fiber: 1g

- Carbohydrates: 45g

Salted Caramel Pretzel Ice Cream

Time to Prepare: 20 minutes
Ninja Creami Time: 5 minutes
Number of Servings: 4

Ingredients

- 1 cup of heavy cream
- 1 cup of whole milk
- 3/4 cup granulated sugar
- 1/2 cup of caramel sauce
- 1/2 teaspoon of sea salt
- 1 teaspoon of vanilla extract
- 1 cup of crushed pretzels

Instructions List:

1. In a medium bowl, whisk together the heavy cream, whole milk, granulated sugar, caramel sauce, sea salt, and vanilla extract until the sugar is dissolved.
2. Pour the mixture into the Ninja Creami Deluxe pint container and secure the lid.
3. Place the container in the freezer and freeze for 24 hours.
4. After freezing, remove the container from the freezer and place it into the Ninja Creami Deluxe machine.
5. Select the "Ice Cream" function and start the machine.
6. Once the cycle is complete, remove the pint container from the machine and create a well in the center of the ice cream.
7. Add the crushed pretzels into the well.
8. Place the pint container back into the Ninja Creami Deluxe and select the "Mix-in" function.
9. Once the mix-in cycle is complete, remove the container and serve immediately.

Nutritional Information (per serving)

- Calories: 420
- Protein: 5g
- Total Fats: 25g
- Fiber: 1g
- Carbohydrates: 45g

Toasted Marshmallow and Graham Cracker Crumble

Time to Prepare: 25 minutes
Ninja Creami Time: 5 minutes
Number of Servings: 4

Ingredients

- 1 cup of heavy cream
- 1 cup of whole milk
- 3/4 cup granulated sugar
- 1 teaspoon of vanilla extract

- 1 cup of mini marshmallows
- 1/2 cup of graham cracker crumbs

Instructions List:

1. In a medium bowl, whisk together the heavy cream, whole milk, granulated sugar, and vanilla extract until the sugar is dissolved.

2. Pour the mixture into the Ninja Creami Deluxe pint container and secure the lid.

3. Place the container in the freezer and freeze for 24 hours.

4. Preheat the broiler in your oven. Spread the mini marshmallows on a baking sheet lined with parchment paper and broil until toasted, watching closely to avoid burning.

5. After freezing, remove the pint container from the freezer and place it into the Ninja Creami Deluxe machine.

6. Select the "Ice Cream" function and start the machine.

7. Once the cycle is complete, remove the pint container from the machine.

8. Create a well in the center of the ice cream and add the toasted marshmallows and graham cracker crumbs.

9. Place the pint container back into the Ninja Creami Deluxe and select the "Mix-in" function.

10. Once the mix-in cycle is complete, remove the container and serve immediately.

Nutritional Information (per serving)

- Calories: 400
- Protein: 5g
- Total Fats: 22g
- Fiber: 1g
- Carbohydrates: 45g

Maple Bacon Ice Cream

Time to Prepare: 30 minutes
Ninja Creami Time: 5 minutes
Number of Servings: 4

Ingredients

- 1 cup of heavy cream
- 1 cup of whole milk
- 3/4 cup maple syrup
- 1/2 cup of granulated sugar
- 1 teaspoon of vanilla extract
- 1/2 cup of cooked bacon, finely chopped

Instructions List:

1. In a medium bowl, whisk together the heavy cream, whole milk, maple syrup, granulated sugar, and vanilla extract until the sugar is dissolved.

2. Pour the mixture into the Ninja Creami Deluxe pint container and secure the lid.

3. Place the container in the freezer and freeze for 24 hours.

4. After freezing, remove the container from the freezer and place it into the Ninja Creami Deluxe machine.

5. Select the "Ice Cream" function and start the machine.

6. Once the cycle is complete, remove the pint container from the machine.

7. Create a well in the center of the ice cream and add the chopped bacon.

8. Place the pint container back into the Ninja Creami Deluxe and select the "Mix-in" function.

9. Once the mix-in cycle is complete, remove the container and serve immediately.

Nutritional Information (per serving)

- Calories: 380

- Protein: 5g

- Total Fats: 24g

- Fiber: 0g

- Carbohydrates: 37g

Candied Pecans and Maple Syrup
Time to Prepare: 25 minutes
Ninja Creami Time: 5 minutes
Number of Servings: 4

Ingredients

- 1 cup of heavy cream

- 1 cup of whole milk

- 3/4 cup granulated sugar

- 1 teaspoon of vanilla extract

- 1/2 cup of maple syrup

- 1/2 cup of candied pecans, chopped

Instructions List:

1. In a medium bowl, whisk together the heavy cream, whole milk, granulated sugar, vanilla extract, and maple syrup until the sugar is dissolved.

2. Pour the mixture into the Ninja Creami Deluxe pint container and secure the lid.

3. Place the container in the freezer and freeze for 24 hours.

4. After freezing, remove the pint container from the freezer and place it into the Ninja Creami Deluxe machine.

5. Select the "Ice Cream" function and start the machine.

6. Once the cycle is complete, remove the pint container from the machine.

7. Create a well in the center of the ice cream and add the chopped candied pecans.

8. Place the pint container back into the Ninja Creami Deluxe and select the "Mix-in" function.

9. Once the mix-in cycle is complete, remove the container and serve immediately.

Nutritional Information (per serving)

- Calories: 450

- Protein: 5g

- Total Fats: 26g

- Fiber: 1g

- Carbohydrates: 50g

Dark Chocolate Chunks and Raspberry Swirl

Time to Prepare: 25 minutes
Ninja Creami Time: 5 minutes
Number of Servings: 4

Ingredients

- 1 cup of heavy cream

- 1 cup of whole milk

- 3/4 cup granulated sugar

- 1 teaspoon of vanilla extract

- 1/2 cup of dark chocolate chunks

- 1/2 cup of raspberry preserves

Instructions List:

1. In a medium bowl, whisk together the heavy cream, whole milk, granulated sugar, and vanilla extract until the sugar is dissolved.

2. Pour the mixture into the Ninja Creami Deluxe pint container and secure the lid.

3. Place the container in the freezer and freeze for 24 hours.

4. After freezing, remove the pint container from the freezer and place it into the Ninja Creami Deluxe machine.

5. Select the "Ice Cream" function and start the machine.

6. Once the cycle is complete, remove the pint container from the machine.

7. Create a well in the center of the ice cream and add the dark chocolate chunks and raspberry preserves.

8. Place the pint container back into the Ninja Creami Deluxe and select the "Mix-in" function.

9. Once the mix-in cycle is complete, remove the container and serve immediately.

Nutritional Information (per serving)

- Calories: 430

- Protein: 6g

- Total Fats: 28g

- Fiber: 2g

- Carbohydrates: 38g

Crushed Butterfinger and Peanut Butter Ribbon

Time to Prepare: 25 minutes
Ninja Creami Time: 5 minutes
Number of Servings: 4

Ingredients

- 1 cup of heavy cream

- 1 cup of whole milk

- 3/4 cup granulated sugar

- 1 teaspoon of vanilla extract

- 1/2 cup of crushed Butterfinger candy

- 1/4 cup of creamy peanut butter, slightly melted

Instructions List:

1. In a medium bowl, whisk together the heavy cream, whole milk, granulated sugar, and vanilla extract until the sugar is dissolved.

2. Pour the mixture into the Ninja Creami Deluxe pint container and secure the lid.

3. Place the container in the freezer and freeze for 24 hours.

4. After freezing, remove the pint container from the freezer and place it into the Ninja Creami Deluxe machine.

5. Select the "Ice Cream" function and start the machine.

6. Once the cycle is complete, remove the pint container from the machine.

7. Create a well in the center of the ice cream and add the crushed Butterfinger candy and melted peanut butter.

8. Place the pint container back into the Ninja Creami Deluxe and select the "Mix-in" function.

9. Once the mix-in cycle is complete, remove the container and serve immediately.

Nutritional Information (per serving)

- Calories: 480

- Protein: 8g

- Total Fats: 30g

- Fiber: 1g

- Carbohydrates: 45g

White Chocolate Chips and Cranberry Sauce

Time to Prepare: 25 minutes
Ninja Creami Time: 5 minutes
Number of Servings: 4

Ingredients

- 1 cup of heavy cream
- 1 cup of whole milk
- 3/4 cup granulated sugar
- 1 teaspoon of vanilla extract
- 1/2 cup of white chocolate chips
- 1/2 cup of cranberry sauce

Instructions List:

1. In a medium bowl, whisk together the heavy cream, whole milk, granulated sugar, and vanilla extract until the sugar is dissolved.
2. Pour the mixture into the Ninja Creami Deluxe pint container and secure the lid.
3. Place the container in the freezer and freeze for 24 hours.
4. After freezing, remove the pint container from the freezer and place it into the Ninja Creami Deluxe machine.
5. Select the "Ice Cream" function and start the machine.
6. Once the cycle is complete, remove the pint container from the machine.
7. Create a well in the center of the ice cream and add the white chocolate chips and cranberry sauce.
8. Place the pint container back into the Ninja Creami Deluxe and select the "Mix-in" function.
9. Once the mix-in cycle is complete, remove the container and serve immediately.

Nutritional Information (per serving)

- Calories: 420
- Protein: 5g
- Total Fats: 26g
- Fiber: 1g
- Carbohydrates: 40g

Cinnamon Sugar Churro Bites

Time to Prepare: 25 minutes
Ninja Creami Time: 5 minutes
Number of Servings: 4

Ingredients

- 1 cup of heavy cream
- 1 cup of whole milk
- 3/4 cup granulated sugar
- 1 teaspoon of vanilla extract
- 1 teaspoon of ground cinnamon
- 1/2 cup of churro bites (pre-cooked and chopped)
- 1/4 cup of cinnamon sugar mixture (1 tablespoon of ground cinnamon + 3 tablespoons granulated sugar)

Instructions List:

1. In a medium bowl, whisk together the heavy cream, whole milk, granulated sugar, vanilla extract, and ground cinnamon until the sugar is dissolved.
2. Pour the mixture into the Ninja Creami Deluxe pint container and secure the lid.
3. Place the container in the freezer and freeze for 24 hours.
4. After freezing, remove the pint container from the freezer and place it into the Ninja Creami Deluxe machine.
5. Select the "Ice Cream" function and start the machine.
6. Once the cycle is complete, remove the pint container from the machine.
7. Create a well in the center of the ice cream and add the chopped churro bites and cinnamon sugar mixture.
8. Place the pint container back into the Ninja Creami Deluxe and select the "Mix-in" function.
9. Once the mix-in cycle is complete, remove the container and serve immediately.

Nutritional Information (per serving)

- Calories: 440
- Protein: 5g
- Total Fats: 28g
- Fiber: 1g
- Carbohydrates: 44g

Blueberry Compote and Lemon Zest

Time to Prepare: 25 minutes
Ninja Creami Time: 5 minutes
Number of Servings: 4

Ingredients

- 1 cup of heavy cream
- 1 cup of whole milk
- 3/4 cup granulated sugar

- 1 teaspoon of vanilla extract

- 1/2 cup of blueberry compote

- Zest of 1 lemon

Instructions List:

1. In a medium bowl, whisk together the heavy cream, whole milk, granulated sugar, and vanilla extract until the sugar is dissolved.

2. Pour the mixture into the Ninja Creami Deluxe pint container and secure the lid.

3. Place the container in the freezer and freeze for 24 hours.

4. After freezing, remove the pint container from the freezer and place it into the Ninja Creami Deluxe machine.

5. Select the "Ice Cream" function and start the machine.

6. Once the cycle is complete, remove the pint container from the machine.

7. Create a well in the center of the ice cream and add the blueberry compote and lemon zest.

8. Place the pint container back into the Ninja Creami Deluxe and select the "Mix-in" function.

9. Once the mix-in cycle is complete, remove the container and serve immediately.

Nutritional Information (per serving)

- Calories: 410

- Protein: 5g

- Total Fats: 26g

- Fiber: 1g

- Carbohydrates: 38g

Bacon Bits and Maple Syrup

Time to Prepare: 25 minutes
Ninja Creami Time: 5 minutes
Number of Servings: 4

Ingredients

- 1 cup of heavy cream

- 1 cup of whole milk

- 3/4 cup granulated sugar

- 1 teaspoon of vanilla extract

- 1/2 cup of cooked bacon bits

- 1/4 cup of maple syrup

Instructions List:

1. In a medium bowl, whisk together the heavy cream, whole milk, granulated sugar, and vanilla extract until the sugar is dissolved.

2. Pour the mixture into the Ninja Creami Deluxe pint container and secure the lid.

3. Place the container in the freezer and freeze for 24 hours.

4. After freezing, remove the pint container from the freezer and place it into the Ninja Creami Deluxe machine.

5. Select the "Ice Cream" function and start the machine.

6. Once the cycle is complete, remove the pint container from the machine.

7. Create a well in the center of the ice cream and add the bacon bits and maple syrup.

8. Place the pint container back into the Ninja Creami Deluxe and select the "Mix-in" function.

9. Once the mix-in cycle is complete, remove the container and serve immediately.

Nutritional Information (per serving)

- Calories: 440
- Protein: 6g
- Total Fats: 28g
- Fiber: 0g
- Carbohydrates: 38g

Chapter 3: Milkshakes

S'mores Milkshake

Time to Prepare: 10 minutes **Ninja Creami Time:** 60 seconds **Servings:** 2-3

Ingredients:

- 1 cup of chocolate ice cream (store-bought or homemade)
- 1/2 cup of milk
- 1/4 cup of marshmallow creme
- 4 graham crackers, crushed (store-bought or homemade)
- 1/4 cup of mini marshmallows

Instructions List:

1. In a bowl, combine chocolate ice cream pieces, milk, and marshmallow creme. Fold in crushed graham crackers and mini marshmallows.

2. Pour the mixture into a Ninja Creami Pint Container and freeze for a minimum of 4 hours, or until the mixture reaches a soft serve consistency.

To Serve:

1. Attach the Ice Cream Spindle to the Ninja Creami Deluxe base unit. Place frozen mixture in the container and secure the lid.

2. Select the "Milkshake" function and press "Start."

3. Enjoy your S'mores Milkshake immediately after bringing it out.

Nutritional Information (per serving, estimated):

- Calories: 450
- Protein: 5g
- Total Fats: 20g
- Fiber: 1g (from graham crackers)
- Carbohydrates: 50g

Caramel Apple Pie Milkshake

Time to Prepare: 10 minutes **Ninja Creami Time:** 60 seconds **Servings:** 2-3

Ingredients:

- 1 cup of vanilla ice cream (store-bought or homemade)
- 1/2 cup of diced, peeled apple (about 1 small apple)
- 1/4 cup of apple cider
- 1/4 cup of caramel sauce
- 1/2 teaspoon of ground cinnamon

- Pinch of nutmeg (optional)

Instructions List:

1. In a blender, combine vanilla ice cream, diced apple, apple cider, caramel sauce, cinnamon, and nutmeg (if using). Blend until smooth and creamy.

2. Pour the mixture into a Ninja Creami Pint Container and freeze for a minimum of 4 hours, or until the mixture reaches a soft serve consistency.

To Serve:

1. Attach the Ice Cream Spindle to the Ninja Creami Deluxe base unit. Place frozen mixture in the container and secure the lid.

2. Select the "Milkshake" function and press "Start."

3. Enjoy your Caramel Apple Pie Milkshake immediately after bringing it out.

Nutritional Information (per serving, estimated):

- Calories: 400

- Protein: 4g

- Total Fats: 15g

- Fiber: 1g (from apple)

- Carbohydrates: 50g

Espresso Oreo Milkshake

Time to Prepare: 10 minutes **Ninja Creami Time:** 60 seconds **Servings:** 2-3

Ingredients:

- 1 cup of vanilla ice cream (store-bought or homemade)

- 1/2 cup of milk

- 1 shot espresso (cooled, or strong brewed coffee)

- 8 Oreo cookies, chopped

- 1 tablespoon of chocolate syrup (optional)

Instructions List:

1. In a blender, combine vanilla ice cream, milk, espresso, and chopped Oreos. Blend until smooth and creamy.

2. For a richer chocolate flavor, drizzle in chocolate syrup and blend again (optional).

3. Pour the mixture into a Ninja Creami Pint Container and freeze for a minimum of 4 hours, or until the mixture reaches a soft serve consistency.

To Serve:

1. Attach the Ice Cream Spindle to the Ninja Creami Deluxe base unit. Place frozen mixture in the container and secure the lid.

2. Select the "Milkshake" function and press "Start."

3. Enjoy your Espresso Oreo Milkshake immediately after bringing it out.

Nutritional Information (per serving, estimated):

- Calories: 450
- Protein: 5g
- Total Fats: 20g
- Fiber: 1g (from Oreos)
- Carbohydrates: 50g

Mango Lassi Milkshake

Time to Prepare: 10 minutes **Ninja Creami Time:** 60 seconds **Servings:** 2-3

Ingredients:

- 1 cup of fresh or frozen mango chunks
- 1/2 cup of plain yogurt
- 1/4 cup of milk (dairy or non-dairy)
- 1/4 teaspoon of ground cardamom (optional)
- Pinch of ground ginger (optional)
- Honey or maple syrup (to taste, optional)

Instructions List:

1. In a blender, combine mango chunks, yogurt, milk, cardamom (if using), and ginger (if using). Blend until smooth and creamy. If the mixture is too thick, add a tablespoon of milk at a time until desired consistency is reached.
2. Taste and adjust sweetness with honey or maple syrup, if desired.
3. Pour the mixture into a Ninja Creami Pint Container and freeze for a minimum of 4 hours, or until the mixture reaches a soft serve consistency.

To Serve:

1. Attach the Ice Cream Spindle to the Ninja Creami Deluxe base unit. Place frozen mixture in the container and secure the lid.
2. Select the "Milkshake" function and press "Start."
3. Enjoy your Mango Lassi Milkshake immediately after bringing it out.

Nutritional Information (per serving, estimated):

- Calories: 300
- Protein: 8g (from yogurt)
- Total Fats: 5g (from yogurt)
- Fiber: 1g (from mango)
- Carbohydrates: 40g

Red Velvet Cake Milkshake

Time to Prepare: 10 minutes **Ninja Creami Time:** 60 seconds **Servings:** 2-3

Ingredients:

- 1 cup of red velvet cake (store-bought or leftover, cubed)
- 1/2 cup of milk
- 1/4 cup of cream cheese frosting
- 1/4 teaspoon of vanilla extract
- Pinch of red food coloring (optional)

Instructions List:

1. In a blender, combine red velvet cake cubes, milk, cream cheese frosting, and vanilla extract. Blend until smooth and creamy. If the mixture is too thick, add a tablespoon of milk at a time until desired consistency is reached.

2. Add a pinch of red food coloring (optional) for a more vibrant red color.

3. Pour the mixture into a Ninja Creami Pint Container and freeze for a minimum of 4 hours, or until the mixture reaches a soft serve consistency.

To Serve:

1. Attach the Ice Cream Spindle to the Ninja Creami Deluxe base unit. Place frozen mixture in the container and secure the lid.

2. Select the "Milkshake" function and press "Start."

3. Enjoy your Red Velvet Cake Milkshake immediately after bringing it out.

Nutritional Information (per serving, estimated):

- Calories: 500
- Protein: 5g
- Total Fats: 30g
- Fiber: 1g (from cake)
- Carbohydrates: 55g

Pumpkin Spice Milkshake

Time to Prepare: 10 minutes **Ninja Creami Time:** 60 seconds **Servings:** 2-3

Ingredients:

- 1 cup of vanilla ice cream (store-bought or homemade)
- 1/2 cup of canned pumpkin puree
- 1/4 cup of milk
- 1/4 cup of pumpkin spice latte syrup (or maple syrup to taste)

- 1/2 teaspoon of ground cinnamon
- Pinch of nutmeg

Instructions List:

1. In a blender, combine vanilla ice cream, pumpkin puree, milk, pumpkin spice latte syrup (or maple syrup), cinnamon, and nutmeg. Blend until smooth and creamy.

2. Pour the mixture into a Ninja Creami Pint Container and freeze for a minimum of 4 hours, or until the mixture reaches a soft serve consistency.

To Serve:

1. Attach the Ice Cream Spindle to the Ninja Creami Deluxe base unit. Place frozen mixture in the container and secure the lid.

2. Select the "Milkshake" function and press "Start."

3. Enjoy your Pumpkin Spice Milkshake immediately after bringing it out.

Nutritional Information (per serving, estimated):

- Calories: 400
- Protein: 4g
- Total Fats: 15g
- Fiber: 1g (from pumpkin)
- Carbohydrates: 50g

Chai Tea Milkshake

Time to Prepare: 10 minutes **Ninja Creami Time:** 60 seconds **Servings:** 2-3

Ingredients:

- 1 cup of chai tea ice cream (store-bought or homemade)
- 1/2 cup of milk (dairy or non-dairy)
- 1/4 cup of brewed chai tea, cooled (or 2 tablespoons chai tea concentrate)
- 1/4 teaspoon of ground cinnamon (optional)
- Pinch of ground ginger (optional)
- Honey or maple syrup (to taste, optional)

Instructions List:

1. In a blender, combine chai tea ice cream, milk, cooled chai tea, cinnamon (if using), and ginger (if using). Blend until smooth and creamy.

2. Taste and adjust sweetness with honey or maple syrup, if desired.

3. Pour the mixture into a Ninja Creami Pint Container and freeze for a minimum of 4 hours, or until the mixture reaches a soft serve consistency.

To Serve:

1. Attach the Ice Cream Spindle to the Ninja Creami Deluxe base unit. Place frozen mixture in the container and secure the lid.

2. Select the "Milkshake" function and press "Start."

3. Enjoy your Chai Tea Milkshake immediately after bringing it out.

Nutritional Information (per serving, estimated):

- Calories: 400

- Protein: 4g (from ice cream)

- Total Fats: 20g (from ice cream)

- Fiber: 1g (trace amounts from chai spices)

- Carbohydrates: 45g (from ice cream)

Nutella Banana Milkshake

Time to Prepare: 5 minutes **Ninja Creami Time:** 60 seconds **Servings:** 2

Ingredients:

- 1 frozen banana, sliced

- 2 tablespoons Nutella

- 1/2 cup of milk (dairy or non-dairy)

- 1/4 cup of vanilla ice cream (optional)

Instructions List:

1. In a blender, combine frozen banana slices, Nutella, and milk. Blend until smooth and creamy.

2. For a thicker and richer milkshake, add vanilla ice cream and blend again until desired consistency is reached (optional).

To Serve:

1. Pour the mixture into a Ninja Creami Pint Container and freeze for a minimum of 2 hours, or until the mixture reaches a soft serve consistency (if using ice cream, this step may not be necessary).

2. Attach the Ice Cream Spindle to the Ninja Creami Deluxe base unit. Place frozen mixture in the container and secure the lid.

3. Select the "Milkshake" function and press "Start."

4. Enjoy your Nutella Banana Milkshake immediately after bringing it out.

Nutritional Information (per serving, estimated):

- Calories: 350

- Protein: 4g (from banana and ice cream, if used)

- Total Fats: 15g (from Nutella and ice cream, if used)

- Fiber: 1g (from banana)

- Carbohydrates: 40g (from banana, Nutella, and ice cream, if used)

Key Lime Pie Milkshake

Time to Prepare: 10 minutes **Ninja Creami Time:** 60 seconds **Servings:** 2-3

Ingredients:

- 1 cup of key lime pie ice cream (store-bought or homemade)
- 1/2 cup of milk (dairy or non-dairy)
- 1/4 cup of graham cracker crumbs
- 1 tablespoon of lime juice
- Whipped cream, for garnish (optional)
- Maraschino cherry, for garnish (optional)

Instructions List:

1. In a blender, combine key lime pie ice cream, milk, graham cracker crumbs, and lime juice. Blend until smooth and creamy.
2. Pour the mixture into a Ninja Creami Pint Container and freeze for a minimum of 4 hours, or until the mixture reaches a soft serve consistency.

To Serve:

1. Attach the Ice Cream Spindle to the Ninja Creami Deluxe base unit. Place frozen mixture in the container and secure the lid.
2. Select the "Milkshake" function and press "Start."
3. Pour into glasses and garnish with whipped cream and a maraschino cherry (optional).
4. Enjoy your Key Lime Pie Milkshake immediately after bringing it out.

Nutritional Information (per serving, estimated):

- Calories: 450
- Protein: 4g (from ice cream)
- Total Fats: 20g (from ice cream)
- Fiber: 1g (from graham crackers)
- Carbohydrates: 50g (from ice cream, graham crackers)

Chocolate Covered Strawberry Milkshake

Time to Prepare: 5 minutes **Ninja Creami Time:** 60 seconds **Servings:** 2

Ingredients:

- 1 cup of fresh or frozen strawberries
- 1/2 cup of milk (dairy or non-dairy)
- 2 tablespoons chocolate syrup
- 1/4 cup of vanilla ice cream (optional)

- 2 tablespoons whipped cream, for garnish (optional)

Instructions List:

1. In a blender, combine strawberries, milk, and chocolate syrup. Blend until smooth and creamy.

2. For a thicker and richer milkshake, add vanilla ice cream and blend again until desired consistency is reached (optional).

To Serve:

1. Pour the mixture into a Ninja Creami Pint Container and freeze for a minimum of 2 hours, or until the mixture reaches a soft serve consistency (if using ice cream, this step may not be necessary).

2. Attach the Ice Cream Spindle to the Ninja Creami Deluxe base unit. Place frozen mixture in the container and secure the lid.

3. Select the "Milkshake" function and press "Start."

4. Pour into glasses and garnish with whipped cream (optional).

5. Enjoy your Chocolate Covered Strawberry Milkshake immediately after bringing it out.

Nutritional Information (per serving, estimated):

- Calories: 300

- Protein: 3g (from ice cream, if used)

- Total Fats: 10g (from ice cream and chocolate syrup, if used)

- Fiber: 2g (from strawberries)

- Carbohydrates: 40g (from strawberries, ice cream, and chocolate syrup, if used)

Pineapple Upside-Down Milkshake

Time to Prepare: 10 minutes **Ninja Creami Time:** 60 seconds **Servings:** 2-3

Ingredients:

- 1 cup of vanilla ice cream (store-bought or homemade)

- 1/2 cup of pineapple chunks (fresh or frozen)

- 1/4 cup of maraschino cherries, halved

- 1/4 cup of pineapple juice

- 1 tablespoon of brown sugar

Instructions List:

1. In a blender, combine vanilla ice cream, pineapple chunks, maraschino cherries, pineapple juice, and brown sugar. Blend until smooth and creamy.

2. Pour the mixture into a Ninja Creami Pint Container and freeze for a minimum of 4 hours, or until the mixture reaches a soft serve consistency.

To Serve:

1. Attach the Ice Cream Spindle to the Ninja Creami Deluxe base unit. Place frozen mixture in the container and secure the lid.

2. Select the "Milkshake" function and press "Start."

3. Enjoy your Pineapple Upside-Down Milkshake immediately after bringing it out.

Nutritional Information (per serving, estimated):

- Calories: 400

- Protein: 4g (from ice cream)

- Total Fats: 15g (from ice cream)

- Fiber: 1g (from pineapple)

- Carbohydrates: 50g (from ice cream, pineapple, and brown sugar)

Salted Caramel Popcorn Milkshake
Time to Prepare: 10 minutes **Ninja Creami Time:** 60 seconds **Servings:** 2-3

Ingredients:

- 1 cup of vanilla ice cream (store-bought or homemade)

- 1/2 cup of milk (dairy or non-dairy)

- 1/4 cup of caramel sauce

- 1/4 cup of salted popcorn, kernels removed (reserve a few tablespoons for garnish)

- Pinch of sea salt (optional)

Instructions List:

1. In a blender, combine vanilla ice cream, milk, caramel sauce, and most of the salted popcorn (reserve a few tablespoons for garnish). Blend until smooth and creamy.

2. Taste and add a pinch of sea salt, if desired, for a more prominent salted caramel flavor.

To Serve:

1. Pour the mixture into a Ninja Creami Pint Container and freeze for a minimum of 4 hours, or until the mixture reaches a soft serve consistency.

2. Attach the Ice Cream Spindle to the Ninja Creami Deluxe base unit. Place frozen mixture in the container and secure the lid.

3. Select the "Milkshake" function and press "Start."

4. Pour into glasses and garnish with reserved salted popcorn.

5. Enjoy your Salted Caramel Popcorn Milkshake immediately!

Nutritional Information (per serving, estimated):

- Calories: 450

- Protein: 4g (from ice cream)

- Total Fats: 20g (from ice cream and caramel sauce)

- Fiber: 1g (from popcorn)

- Carbohydrates: 50g (from ice cream, caramel sauce, and popcorn)

Black Forest Milkshake

Time to Prepare: 10 minutes **Ninja Creami Time:** 60 seconds **Servings:** 2-3

Ingredients:

- 1 cup of chocolate cherry ice cream (store-bought or homemade)
- 1/2 cup of milk (dairy or non-dairy)
- 2 tablespoons maraschino cherries, chopped
- 2 tablespoons cherry syrup
- 1/4 teaspoon of almond extract (optional)
- Whipped cream and maraschino cherry, for garnish (optional)

Instructions List:

1. In a blender, combine chocolate cherry ice cream, milk, chopped maraschino cherries, cherry syrup, and almond extract (if using). Blend until smooth and creamy.

To Serve:

1. Pour the mixture into a Ninja Creami Pint Container and freeze for a minimum of 4 hours, or until the mixture reaches a soft serve consistency.
2. Attach the Ice Cream Spindle to the Ninja Creami Deluxe base unit. Place frozen mixture in the container and secure the lid.
3. Select the "Milkshake" function and press "Start."
4. Pour into glasses and garnish with whipped cream and a maraschino cherry (optional).
5. Enjoy your Black Forest Milkshake immediately after bringing it out.

Nutritional Information (per serving, estimated):

- Calories: 450
- Protein: 4g (from ice cream)
- Total Fats: 20g (from ice cream)
- Fiber: 1g (from trace amounts in cherries)
- Carbohydrates: 50g (from ice cream, cherry syrup, and maraschino cherries)

Lavender Honey Milkshake

Time to Prepare: 5 minutes **Ninja Creami Time:** 60 seconds **Servings:** 2

Ingredients:

- 1 cup of vanilla ice cream (store-bought or homemade)
- 1/2 cup of milk (dairy or non-dairy)
- 1 tablespoon of honey
- 1 teaspoon of dried lavender flowers

- Pinch of sea salt (optional)

Instructions List:

1. In a blender, combine vanilla ice cream, milk, honey, and dried lavender flowers. Blend until smooth and creamy. If the mixture is too thick, add a tablespoon of milk at a time until desired consistency is reached.

2. Taste and add a pinch of sea salt, if desired, to enhance the floral and honey flavors.

To Serve:

1. Pour the mixture into a Ninja Creami Pint Container and freeze for a minimum of 2 hours, or until the mixture reaches a soft serve consistency.

2. Attach the Ice Cream Spindle to the Ninja Creami Deluxe base unit. Place frozen mixture in the container and secure the lid.

3. Select the "Milkshake" function and press "Start."

4. Enjoy your Lavender Honey Milkshake immediately after bringing it out.

Nutritional Information (per serving, estimated):

- Calories: 350

- Protein: 4g (from ice cream)

- Total Fats: 15g (from ice cream)

- Fiber: 1g (trace amounts)

- Carbohydrates: 40g (from ice cream, honey, and milk)

Chapter 4: Creamiccinos

Classic Vanilla Bean Creamiccino

Time to Prepare: 5 minutes **Ninja Creami Time:** 60 seconds **Servings:** 1

Ingredients:

- 200g (3/4 cup) sweetened condensed milk
- 60g (1/4 cup) water
- 1 teaspoon of vanilla bean paste (or 1/2 vanilla bean, scraped)

Instructions List:

1. In a Ninja Creami Pint Container, combine sweetened condensed milk, water, and vanilla bean paste (or scraped vanilla bean). Stir well to combine.

To Serve:

1. **Freeze for at least 4 hours, or overnight, until the mixture reaches a slushy consistency.**
2. Attach the Creamerizer Paddle to the Ninja Creami Deluxe base unit. Place frozen mixture in the container and secure the lid.
3. Select the "Creamiccino" function and press "Start."
4. Enjoy your Classic Vanilla Bean Creamiccino immediately after bringing it out.

Nutritional Information (per serving, estimated):

- Calories: 320
- Protein: 3g
- Total Fats: 10g
- Fiber: 0g
- Carbohydrates: 45g

Mocha Hazelnut Creamiccino

Time to Prepare: 5 minutes **Ninja Creami Time:** 60 seconds **Servings:** 1

Ingredients:

- 115g (1/2 cup) strong brewed coffee, cooled (or cold brew)
- 60g (1/4 cup) hazelnut liqueur (such as Frangelico)
- 2 tablespoons chocolate syrup
- 1 tablespoon of milk (dairy or non-dairy)

Instructions List:

1. In a Ninja Creami Pint Container, combine cooled coffee, hazelnut liqueur, chocolate syrup, and milk. Stir well to combine.

To Serve:

1. **Freeze for at least 4 hours, or overnight, until the mixture reaches a slushy consistency.**

2. Attach the Creamerizer Paddle to the Ninja Creami Deluxe base unit. Place frozen mixture in the container and secure the lid.

3. Select the "Creamiccino" function and press "Start."

4. Enjoy your Mocha Hazelnut Creamiccino immediately after bringing it out.

Nutritional Information (per serving, estimated):

- Calories: 250

- Protein: 1g

- Total Fats: 5g

- Fiber: 0g

- Carbohydrates: 30g

Caramel Macchiato Creamiccino

Time to Prepare: 5 minutes **Ninja Creami Time:** 60 seconds **Servings:** 1

Ingredients:

- 115g (1/2 cup) strong brewed coffee, cooled (or cold brew)

- 60g (1/4 cup) milk (dairy or non-dairy)

- 2 tablespoons caramel sauce

- 1 tablespoon of sugar (optional)

Instructions List:

1. In a Ninja Creami Pint Container, combine cooled coffee, milk, and caramel sauce. Stir well to combine. Taste and add sugar, if desired, for a sweeter flavor.

To Serve:

1. **Freeze for at least 4 hours, or overnight, until the mixture reaches a slushy consistency.**

2. Attach the Creamerizer Paddle to the Ninja Creami Deluxe base unit. Place frozen mixture in the container and secure the lid.

3. Select the "Creamiccino" function and press "Start."

4. Enjoy your Caramel Macchiato Creamiccino immediately after bringing it out.

Nutritional Information (per serving, estimated):

- Calories: 200

- Protein: 2g (from milk)

- Total Fats: 4g (from milk)

- Fiber: 0g

- Carbohydrates: 25g (from coffee, milk, caramel sauce, and sugar if used)

Pumpkin Spice Creamiccino

Time to Prepare: 5 minutes **Ninja Creami Time:** 60 seconds **Servings:** 1

Ingredients:

- 115g (1/2 cup) strong brewed coffee, cooled (or cold brew)
- 60g (1/4 cup) milk (dairy or non-dairy)
- 2 tablespoons pumpkin puree
- 1/2 teaspoon of pumpkin pie spice
- 1 tablespoon of maple syrup (or to taste)

Instructions List:

1. In a Ninja Creami Pint Container, combine cooled coffee, milk, pumpkin puree, pumpkin pie spice, and maple syrup. Stir well to combine.

To Serve:

1. **Freeze for at least 4 hours, or overnight, until the mixture reaches a slushy consistency.**
2. Attach the Creamerizer Paddle to the Ninja Creami Deluxe base unit. Place frozen mixture in the container and secure the lid.
3. Select the "Creamiccino" function and press "Start."
4. Enjoy your Pumpkin Spice Creamiccino immediately after bringing it out.

Nutritional Information (per serving, estimated):

- Calories: 180
- Protein: 2g (from milk)
- Total Fats: 2g (from milk)
- Fiber: 1g (from pumpkin)
- Carbohydrates: 30g (from coffee, milk, pumpkin puree, maple syrup)

Mint Chocolate Chip Creamiccino

Time to Prepare: 5 minutes **Ninja Creami Time:** 60 seconds **Servings:** 1

Ingredients:

- 115g (1/2 cup) milk (dairy or non-dairy)
- 60g (1/4 cup) strong brewed coffee, cooled (or cold brew)
- 2 tablespoons chocolate syrup
- 1/2 teaspoon of peppermint extract
- 1/4 cup of mini chocolate chips (for mixing in)

Instructions List:

1. In a Ninja Creami Pint Container, combine milk, cooled coffee, chocolate syrup, and peppermint extract. Stir well to combine.

To Serve:

1. Freeze for at least 4 hours, or overnight, until the mixture reaches a slushy consistency.

2. Attach the Creamerizer Paddle to the Ninja Creami Deluxe base unit. Place frozen mixture in the container and secure the lid.

3. Select the "Creamiccino" function and press "Start."

4. After processing, pour the Mint Chocolate Chip Creamiccino into a glass.

5. Fold in the mini chocolate chips using a spoon.

6. Enjoy immediately after bringing it out.

Nutritional Information (per serving, estimated):

- Calories: 250

- Protein: 4g (from milk)

- Total Fats: 8g (from milk and chocolate syrup)

- Fiber: 0g

- Carbohydrates: 30g (from coffee, milk, chocolate syrup, and mini chocolate chips)

Cinnamon Dolce Creamiccino

Time to Prepare: 5 minutes **Ninja Creami Time:** 60 seconds **Servings:** 1

Ingredients:

- 115g (1/2 cup) milk (dairy or non-dairy)

- 60g (1/4 cup) strong brewed coffee, cooled (or cold brew)

- 2 tablespoons cinnamon dolce syrup (or 1 tablespoon of ground cinnamon + 1 tablespoon of sugar)

- 1/4 teaspoon of vanilla extract

Instructions List:

1. In a Ninja Creami Pint Container, combine milk, cooled coffee, cinnamon dolce syrup (or cinnamon and sugar mixture), and vanilla extract. Stir well to combine.

To Serve:

1. Freeze for at least 4 hours, or overnight, until the mixture reaches a slushy consistency.

2. Attach the Creamerizer Paddle to the Ninja Creami Deluxe base unit. Place frozen mixture in the container and secure the lid.

3. Select the "Creamiccino" function and press "Start."

4. Enjoy your Cinnamon Dolce Creamiccino immediately after bringing it out.

Nutritional Information (per serving, estimated):

- Calories: 200

- Protein: 4g (from milk)

- Total Fats: 4g (from milk)

- Fiber: 0g
- Carbohydrates: 25g (from coffee, milk, cinnamon dolce syrup (or sugar if used))

Lavender Honey Creamiccino

Time to Prepare: 5 minutes **Ninja Creami Time:** 60 seconds **Servings:** 1

Ingredients:

- 115g (1/2 cup) milk (dairy or non-dairy)
- 60g (1/4 cup) strong brewed coffee, cooled (or cold brew)
- 1 tablespoon of honey
- 1 teaspoon of dried lavender flowers

Instructions List:

1. In a Ninja Creami Pint Container, combine milk, cooled coffee, honey, and dried lavender flowers. Stir well to combine.

To Serve:

1. Freeze for at least 4 hours, or overnight, until the mixture reaches a slushy consistency.
2. Attach the Creamerizer Paddle to the Ninja Creami Deluxe base unit. Place frozen mixture in the container and secure the lid.
3. Select the "Creamiccino" function and press "Start."
4. Enjoy your Lavender Honey Creamiccino immediately after bringing it out.

Nutritional Information (per serving, estimated):

- Calories: 180
- Protein: 2g (from milk)
- Total Fats: 2g (from milk)
- Fiber: 0g
- Carbohydrates: 25g (from coffee, milk, and honey)

Peanut Butter Mocha Creamiccino

Time to Prepare: 5 minutes **Ninja Creami Time:** 60 seconds **Servings:** 1

Ingredients:

- 115g (1/2 cup) milk (dairy or non-dairy)
- 60g (1/4 cup) strong brewed coffee, cooled (or cold brew)
- 2 tablespoons chocolate syrup
- 1 tablespoon of peanut butter (creamy or chunky)

Instructions List:

1. In a Ninja Creami Pint Container, combine milk, cooled coffee, and chocolate syrup. Stir well to combine.

2. Add the peanut butter and stir until evenly distributed (chunky peanut butter will have visible peanut pieces).

To Serve:

1. **Freeze for at least 4 hours, or overnight, until the mixture reaches a slushy consistency.**

2. Attach the Creamerizer Paddle to the Ninja Creami Deluxe base unit. Place frozen mixture in the container and secure the lid.

3. Select the "Creamiccino" function and press "Start."

4. Enjoy your Peanut Butter Mocha Creamiccino immediately after bringing it out.

Nutritional Information (per serving, estimated):

- Calories: 300

- Protein: 8g (from milk and peanut butter)

- Total Fats: 12g (from milk, chocolate syrup, and peanut butter)

- Fiber: 2g (from peanut butter)

- Carbohydrates: 30g (from coffee, milk, chocolate syrup, and peanut butter)

Coconut Caramel Creamiccino

Time to Prepare: 5 minutes **Ninja Creami Time:** 60 seconds **Servings:** 1

Ingredients:

- 115g (1/2 cup) unsweetened coconut milk

- 60g (1/4 cup) strong brewed coffee, cooled (or cold brew)

- 2 tablespoons caramel sauce

- 1/2 teaspoon of vanilla extract

Instructions List:

1. In a Ninja Creami Pint Container, combine coconut milk, cooled coffee, caramel sauce, and vanilla extract. Stir well to combine.

To Serve:

1. **Freeze for at least 4 hours, or overnight, until the mixture reaches a slushy consistency.**

2. Attach the Creamerizer Paddle to the Ninja Creami Deluxe base unit. Place frozen mixture in the container and secure the lid.

3. Select the "Creamiccino" function and press "Start."

4. Enjoy your Coconut Caramel Creamiccino immediately after bringing it out.

Nutritional Information (per serving, estimated):

- Calories: 180

- Protein: 1g (from coconut milk)

- Total Fats: 7g (from coconut milk and caramel sauce)

- Fiber: 1g (from coconut milk)

- Carbohydrates: 25g (from coffee, coconut milk, and caramel sauce)

Maple Pecan Creamiccino

Time to Prepare: 5 minutes **Ninja Creami Time:** 60 seconds **Servings:** 1

Ingredients:

- 115g (1/2 cup) milk (dairy or non-dairy)

- 60g (1/4 cup) strong brewed coffee, cooled (or cold brew)

- 2 tablespoons maple syrup

- 1/4 cup of chopped pecans

- Pinch of ground cinnamon (optional)

Instructions List:

1. In a Ninja Creami Pint Container, combine milk, cooled coffee, maple syrup, and ground cinnamon (if using). Stir well to combine.

2. Fold in the chopped pecans, making sure they are evenly distributed.

To Serve:

1. **Freeze for at least 4 hours, or overnight, until the mixture reaches a slushy consistency.**

2. Attach the Creamerizer Paddle to the Ninja Creami Deluxe base unit. Place frozen mixture in the container and secure the lid.

3. Select the "Creamiccino" function and press "Start."

4. Enjoy your Maple Pecan Creamiccino immediately after bringing it out.

Nutritional Information (per serving, estimated):

- Calories: 300

- Protein: 4g (from milk)

- Total Fats: 10g (from milk and pecans)

- Fiber: 2g (from pecans)

- Carbohydrates: 35g (from coffee, milk, maple syrup, and pecans)

Spiced Chai Creamiccino

Time to Prepare: 5 minutes **Ninja Creami Time:** 60 seconds **Servings:** 1

Ingredients:

- 115g (1/2 cup) milk (dairy or non-dairy)

- 60g (1/4 cup) chai tea latte concentrate (or strongly brewed chai tea, cooled)

- 1 tablespoon of maple syrup (or to taste)

- 1/4 teaspoon of ground cinnamon

Instructions List:

1. In a Ninja Creami Pint Container, combine milk, chai tea latte concentrate (or cooled chai tea), maple syrup, and ground cinnamon. Stir well to combine.

To Serve:

1. **Freeze for at least 4 hours, or overnight, until the mixture reaches a slushy consistency.**

2. Attach the Creamerizer Paddle to the Ninja Creami Deluxe base unit. Place frozen mixture in the container and secure the lid.

3. Select the "Creamiccino" function and press "Start."

4. Enjoy your Spiced Chai Creamiccino immediately after bringing it out.

Nutritional Information (per serving, estimated):

- Calories: 150 (using chai tea latte concentrate) or 100 (using brewed chai tea)

- Protein: 4g (from milk)

- Total Fats: 2g (from milk)

- Fiber: 0g (trace amounts in chai tea)

- Carbohydrates: 20g (from chai tea latte concentrate or brewed chai tea, and maple syrup)

Gingerbread Creamiccino

Time to Prepare: 5 minutes **Ninja Creami Time:** 60 seconds **Servings:** 1

Ingredients:

- 115g (1/2 cup) milk (dairy or non-dairy)

- 60g (1/4 cup) strong brewed coffee, cooled (or cold brew)

- 2 tablespoons molasses

- 1 teaspoon of ground ginger

- 1/2 teaspoon of ground cinnamon

- Pinch of ground nutmeg (optional)

Instructions List:

1. In a Ninja Creami Pint Container, combine milk, cooled coffee, molasses, ground ginger, ground cinnamon, and nutmeg (if using). Stir well to combine.

To Serve:

1. **Freeze for at least 4 hours, or overnight, until the mixture reaches a slushy consistency.**

2. Attach the Creamerizer Paddle to the Ninja Creami Deluxe base unit. Place frozen mixture in the container and secure the lid.

3. Select the "Creamiccino" function and press "Start."

4. Enjoy your Gingerbread Creamiccino immediately after bringing it out.

Nutritional Information (per serving, estimated):

- Calories: 200
- Protein: 4g (from milk)
- Total Fats: 2g (from milk)
- Fiber: 0g (trace amounts)
- Carbohydrates: 30g (from coffee, milk, molasses, and spices)

Chapter 5: Sorbets

Mango Habanero Sorbet

Time to Prepare: 5 minutes **Ninja Creami Time:** 60 seconds **Servings:** 1-2 (depending on spice tolerance)

Ingredients:

- 200g (1 cup) frozen mango chunks
- 60g (1/4 cup) water
- 1-2 tablespoons lime juice (adjust to taste)
- 1/4 habanero pepper, seeded and chopped (adjust for desired spice level)

Instructions List:

1. In a Ninja Creami Pint Container, combine frozen mango chunks, water, lime juice, and habanero pepper.

To Serve:

1. **Freeze for at least 6 hours, or overnight, until completely solid. Warning:** The habanero pepper may slow down the freezing process. Check for solidity before processing.
2. Attach the Multi-Function Blade to the Ninja Creami Deluxe base unit. Place frozen mixture in the container and secure the lid.
3. Select the "Sorbet" function and press "Start."
4. Enjoy your Mango Habanero Sorbet immediately after bringing it out. Start with a small amount to assess the spice level.

Nutritional Information (per serving, estimated):

- Calories: 100
- Protein: 1g (from mango)
- Total Fats: 0g
- Fiber: 2g (from mango)
- Carbohydrates: 24g (from mango)

Raspberry Lime Sorbet

Time to Prepare: 5 minutes **Ninja Creami Time:** 60 seconds **Servings:** 1-2

Ingredients:

- 200g (1 cup) frozen raspberries
- 60g (1/4 cup) water
- 1-2 tablespoons lime juice (adjust to taste)
- 1 tablespoon of agave nectar (or honey)

Instructions List:

1. In a Ninja Creami Pint Container, combine frozen raspberries, water, lime juice, and agave nectar (or honey).

To Serve:

1. **Freeze for at least 6 hours, or overnight, until completely solid.**

2. Attach the Multi-Function Blade to the Ninja Creami Deluxe base unit. Place frozen mixture in the container and secure the lid.

3. Select the "Sorbet" function and press "Start."

4. Enjoy your Raspberry Lime Sorbet immediately after bringing it out.

Nutritional Information (per serving, estimated):

- Calories: 120

- Protein: 1g (from raspberries)

- Total Fats: 0g

- Fiber: 3g (from raspberries)

- Carbohydrates: 28g (from raspberries, lime juice, and agave nectar or honey)

Coconut Pineapple Sorbet

Time to Prepare: 5 minutes **Ninja Creami Time:** 60 seconds **Servings:** 1-2

Ingredients:

- 150g (1 cup) frozen pineapple chunks

- 100g (1/2 cup) canned crushed pineapple (including juice)

- 60g (1/4 cup) coconut milk (full-fat or light)

- 1 tablespoon of lime juice (optional)

Instructions List:

1. In a Ninja Creami Pint Container, combine frozen pineapple chunks, crushed pineapple with juice, coconut milk, and lime juice (if using). Stir well to combine.

To Serve:

1. **Freeze for at least 6 hours, or overnight, until completely solid.**

2. Attach the Multi-Function Blade to the Ninja Creami Deluxe base unit. Place frozen mixture in the container and secure the lid.

3. Select the "Sorbet" function and press "Start."

4. Enjoy your Coconut Pineapple Sorbet immediately after bringing it out.

Nutritional Information (per serving, estimated):

- Calories: 150

- Protein: 1g (from coconut milk)

- Total Fats: 4g (from coconut milk)

- Fiber: 2g (from pineapple)

- Carbohydrates: 28g (from pineapple, coconut milk, and lime juice (if used))

Cucumber Mint Sorbet

Time to Prepare: 5 minutes **Ninja Creami Time:** 60 seconds **Servings:** 1-2

Ingredients:

- 150g (1 cup) peeled and diced cucumber
- 60g (1/4 cup) water
- 1-2 tablespoons lime juice (adjust to taste)
- 10 fresh mint leaves

Instructions List:

1. In a Ninja Creami Pint Container, combine diced cucumber, water, lime juice, and fresh mint leaves.

To Serve:

1. **Freeze for at least 6 hours, or overnight, until completely solid.**
2. Attach the Multi-Function Blade to the Ninja Creami Deluxe base unit. Place frozen mixture in the container and secure the lid.
3. Select the "Sorbet" function and press "Start."
4. Enjoy your Cucumber Mint Sorbet immediately after bringing it out.

Nutritional Information (per serving, estimated):

- Calories: 30
- Protein: 0g
- Total Fats: 0g
- Fiber: 1g (from cucumber)
- Carbohydrates: 7g (from cucumber and lime juice)

Ginger Pear Sorbet

Time to Prepare: 5 minutes **Ninja Creami Time:** 60 seconds **Servings:** 1-2

Ingredients:

- 200g (1 cup) frozen pear chunks
- 60g (1/4 cup) water
- 1-2 tablespoons honey (adjust to taste)
- 1 tablespoon of grated fresh ginger

Instructions List:

1. In a Ninja Creami Pint Container, combine frozen pear chunks, water, honey, and grated ginger.

To Serve:

1. **Freeze for at least 6 hours, or overnight, until completely solid.**

2. Attach the Multi-Function Blade to the Ninja Creami Deluxe base unit. Place frozen mixture in the container and secure the lid.

3. Select the "Sorbet" function and press "Start."

4. Enjoy your Ginger Pear Sorbet immediately after bringing it out.

Nutritional Information (per serving, estimated):

- Calories: 150

- Protein: 1g (from pear)

- Total Fats: 0g

- Fiber: 3g (from pear)

- Carbohydrates: 35g (from pear and honey)

Watermelon Basil Sorbet

Time to Prepare: 5 minutes **Ninja Creami Time:** 60 seconds **Servings:** 1-2

Ingredients:

- 200g (1 cup) seedless watermelon chunks, frozen

- 60g (1/4 cup) water

- 1-2 tablespoons lime juice (adjust to taste)

- 5-10 fresh basil leaves

Instructions List:

1. In a Ninja Creami Pint Container, combine frozen watermelon chunks, water, lime juice, and fresh basil leaves.

To Serve:

1. **Freeze for at least 6 hours, or overnight, until completely solid.**

2. Attach the Multi-Function Blade to the Ninja Creami Deluxe base unit. Place frozen mixture in the container and secure the lid.

3. Select the "Sorbet" function and press "Start."

4. Enjoy your Watermelon Basil Sorbet immediately after bringing it out. Remove any large basil pieces before serving, if desired.

Nutritional Information (per serving, estimated):

- Calories: 80

- Protein: 1g (from watermelon)

- Total Fats: 0g

- Fiber: 1g (from watermelon)

- Carbohydrates: 20g (from watermelon and lime juice)

Strawberry Balsamic Sorbet

Time to Prepare: 5 minutes **Ninja Creami Time:** 60 seconds **Servings:** 1-2

Ingredients:

- 200g (1 cup) frozen strawberries
- 60g (1/4 cup) water
- 1-2 tablespoons honey (adjust to taste)
- 1/2 tablespoon of balsamic vinegar (preferably aged)

Instructions List:

1. In a Ninja Creami Pint Container, combine frozen strawberries, water, honey, and balsamic vinegar.

To Serve:

1. **Freeze for at least 6 hours, or overnight, until completely solid.**
2. Attach the Multi-Function Blade to the Ninja Creami Deluxe base unit. Place frozen mixture in the container and secure the lid.
3. Select the "Sorbet" function and press "Start."
4. Enjoy your Strawberry Balsamic Sorbet immediately after bringing it out. Start with a small amount to assess the tanginess of the balsamic vinegar.

Nutritional Information (per serving, estimated):

- Calories: 130
- Protein: 1g (from strawberries)
- Total Fats: 0g
- Fiber: 2g (from strawberries)
- Carbohydrates: 30g (from strawberries, honey, and balsamic vinegar)

Blood Orange Sorbet

Time to Prepare: 5 minutes **Ninja Creami Time:** 60 seconds **Servings:** 1-2

Ingredients:

- 200g (1 cup) frozen blood orange chunks
- 60g (1/4 cup) water
- 1-2 tablespoons honey (adjust to taste)

Instructions List:

1. In a Ninja Creami Pint Container, combine frozen blood orange chunks, water, and honey.

To Serve:

1. **Freeze for at least 6 hours, or overnight, until completely solid.**
2. Attach the Multi-Function Blade to the Ninja Creami Deluxe base unit. Place frozen mixture in the container and secure the lid.

3. Select the "Sorbet" function and press "Start."

4. Enjoy your Blood Orange Sorbet immediately after bringing it out.

Nutritional Information (per serving, estimated):

- Calories: 120

- Protein: 1g (from blood oranges)

- Total Fats: 0g

- Fiber: 2g (from blood oranges)

- Carbohydrates: 28g (from blood oranges and honey)

Kiwi Lemongrass Sorbet

Time to Prepare: 5 minutes **Ninja Creami Time:** 60 seconds **Servings:** 1-2

Ingredients:

- 200g (1 cup) frozen kiwi chunks

- 60g (1/4 cup) water

- 1-2 tablespoons lime juice (adjust to taste)

- 1 stalk lemongrass, tough outer leaves removed, chopped (or 1/2 teaspoon of lemongrass paste)

Instructions List:

1. In a Ninja Creami Pint Container, combine frozen kiwi chunks, water, lime juice, and chopped lemongrass (or lemongrass paste).

To Serve:

1. **Freeze for at least 6 hours, or overnight, until completely solid.**

2. Attach the Multi-Function Blade to the Ninja Creami Deluxe base unit. Place frozen mixture in the container and secure the lid.

3. Select the "Sorbet" function and press "Start."

4. Enjoy your Kiwi Lemongrass Sorbet immediately after bringing it out. Strain out any large lemongrass pieces before serving, if desired.

Nutritional Information (per serving, estimated):

- Calories: 110

- Protein: 1g (from kiwi)

- Total Fats: 0g

- Fiber: 2g (from kiwi)

- Carbohydrates: 25g (from kiwi and lime juice)

Grapefruit Rosemary Sorbet

Time to Prepare: 5 minutes **Ninja Creami Time:** 60 seconds **Servings:** 1-2

Ingredients:

- 200g (1 cup) frozen grapefruit chunks

- 60g (1/4 cup) water

- 1-2 tablespoons honey (adjust to taste)

- 1 sprig fresh rosemary, leaves removed and chopped (or 1/4 teaspoon of dried rosemary)

Instructions List:

1. In a Ninja Creami Pint Container, combine frozen grapefruit chunks, water, honey, and chopped fresh rosemary (or dried rosemary).

To Serve:

1. **Freeze for at least 6 hours, or overnight, until completely solid.**

2. Attach the Multi-Function Blade to the Ninja Creami Deluxe base unit. Place frozen mixture in the container and secure the lid.

3. Select the "Sorbet" function and press "Start."

4. Enjoy your Grapefruit Rosemary Sorbet immediately after bringing it out. Strain out any large rosemary pieces before serving, if desired.

Nutritional Information (per serving, estimated):

- Calories: 120

- Protein: 1g (from grapefruit)

- Total Fats: 0g

- Fiber: 2g (from grapefruit)

- Carbohydrates: 28g (from grapefruit and honey)

Chapter 6: Gelatos

Stracciatella Gelato

Time to Prepare: 10 minutes **Ninja Creami Time:** 30 minutes **Servings:** 2

Ingredients:

- 2 cups of heavy cream
- 1 cup of whole milk
- 3/4 cup granulated sugar
- 1/4 teaspoon of salt
- 1 1/2 teaspoons of vanilla extract
- 1/2 cup of semisweet chocolate chips

Instructions List:

1. In a saucepan, whisk together heavy cream, milk, sugar, and salt. Heat over medium heat until sugar dissolves and mixture simmers gently around the edges, about 5 minutes. Do not boil.
2. Remove from heat and stir in vanilla extract. Let cool completely, at least 2 hours or overnight in the refrigerator.
3. Once chilled, pour the mixture into the Ninja Creami Pint Container.
4. Attach the Creami Paddle to the Ninja Creami Deluxe base unit. Place the container on the base and secure the lid.
5. Select the "Gelato" function and press "Start." The Ninja Creami will automatically churn the gelato for approximately 30 minutes. During churning, a chime will indicate when to add mix-ins.
6. When the chime sounds, pause the machine and add the chocolate chips. Press "Start" to resume churning until complete.

Nutritional Information (per serving, estimated):

- Calories: 500
- Protein: 5g
- Total Fats: 35g
- Fiber: 0g
- Carbohydrates: 45g

Hazelnut Gelato

Time to Prepare: 15 minutes **Ninja Creami Time:** 30 minutes **Servings:** 2

Ingredients:

- 1 1/2 cups of whole milk
- 1 cup of heavy cream
- 3/4 cup granulated sugar

- 1/4 teaspoon of salt

- 1/2 cup of toasted hazelnuts (plus additional for topping, optional)

- 2 tablespoons hazelnut liqueur (optional)

- 1 teaspoon of vanilla extract

Instructions List:

1. In a saucepan, combine milk, heavy cream, sugar, and salt. Heat over medium heat until sugar dissolves and mixture simmers gently around the edges, about 5 minutes. Do not boil.

2. Remove from heat and stir in toasted hazelnuts. Let mixture steep for 30 minutes to infuse flavor, then strain through a fine-mesh sieve to remove solids. Discard solids or reserve for another use.

3. Stir in hazelnut liqueur (if using) and vanilla extract. Let mixture cool completely, at least 2 hours or overnight in the refrigerator.

4. Once chilled, pour the mixture into the Ninja Creami Pint Container.

5. Attach the Creami Paddle to the Ninja Creami Deluxe base unit. Place the container on the base and secure the lid.

6. Select the "Gelato" function and press "Start." The Ninja Creami will automatically churn the gelato for approximately 30 minutes. During churning, a chime will not indicate adding mix-ins for this recipe.

7. After churning is complete, transfer gelato to a container and freeze for at least 4 hours before scooping. Optionally, sprinkle with additional chopped toasted hazelnuts before freezing.

Nutritional Information (per serving, estimated):

- Calories: 480

- Protein: 5g

- Total Fats: 32g

- Fiber: 1g (from hazelnuts)

- Carbohydrates: 40g (includes sugars from hazelnut liqueur, if used)

Ricotta Fig Gelato

Time to Prepare: 15 minutes **Ninja Creami Time:** 30 minutes **Servings:** 2

Ingredients:

- 1 1/2 cups of whole milk

- 1 cup of ricotta cheese (whole-milk ricotta recommended)

- 3/4 cup granulated sugar

- 1/4 teaspoon of salt

- 1 teaspoon of vanilla extract

- 1/2 cup of chopped fresh figs (or 1/2 cup of dried figs, chopped)

Instructions List:

1. In a saucepan, whisk together milk, ricotta cheese, sugar, and salt. Heat over medium heat until sugar dissolves and mixture simmers gently around the edges, about 5 minutes. Do not boil.

2. Remove from heat and stir in vanilla extract. Let mixture cool slightly, about 20 minutes.

3. Pour the mixture into a blender and blend until smooth. Strain through a fine-mesh sieve to remove any ricotta cheese curds. Discard curds or reserve for another use.

4. Stir in chopped figs. Let mixture cool completely, at least 2 hours or overnight in the refrigerator.

5. Once chilled, pour the mixture into the Ninja Creami Pint Container.

6. Attach the Creami Paddle to the Ninja Creami Deluxe base unit. Place the container on the base and secure the lid.

7. Select the "Gelato" function and press "Start." The Ninja Creami will automatically churn the gelato for approximately 30 minutes. During churning, a chime will not indicate adding mix-ins for this recipe.

8. After churning is complete, transfer gelato to a container and freeze for at least 4 hours before scooping.

Nutritional Information (per serving, estimated):

- Calories: 450
- Protein: 8g (from ricotta cheese)
- Total Fats: 25g (from ricotta cheese)
- Fiber: 2g (from figs)
- Carbohydrates: 40g (includes sugars from milk and figs)

Amaretto Gelato

Time to Prepare: 10 minutes **Ninja Creami Time:** 30 minutes **Servings:** 2

Ingredients:

- 1 1/2 cups of whole milk
- 1 cup of heavy cream
- 3/4 cup granulated sugar
- 1/4 teaspoon of salt
- 2 tablespoons amaretto liqueur
- 1 teaspoon of vanilla extract

Instructions List:

1. In a saucepan, whisk together milk, heavy cream, sugar, and salt. Heat over medium heat until sugar dissolves and mixture simmers gently around the edges, about 5 minutes. Do not boil.

2. Remove from heat and stir in amaretto liqueur and vanilla extract. Let mixture cool completely, at least 2 hours or overnight in the refrigerator.

3. Once chilled, pour the mixture into the Ninja Creami Pint Container.

4. Attach the Creami Paddle to the Ninja Creami Deluxe base unit. Place the container on the base and secure the lid.

5. Select the "Gelato" function and press "Start." The Ninja Creami will automatically churn the gelato for approximately 30 minutes. During churning, a chime will not indicate adding mix-ins for this recipe.

6. After churning is complete, transfer gelato to a container and freeze for at least 4 hours before scooping.

Nutritional Information (per serving, estimated):

- Calories: 480

- Protein: 5g

- Total Fats: 30g

- Fiber: 0g

- Carbohydrates: 45g (includes sugars from amaretto liqueur)

Lemon Basil Gelato

Time to Prepare: 10 minutes **Ninja Creami Time:** 30 minutes **Servings:** 2

Ingredients:

- 1 1/2 cups of whole milk

- 1 cup of heavy cream

- 3/4 cup granulated sugar

- 1/4 teaspoon of salt

- 1/2 cup of fresh basil leaves

- 1/4 cup of lemon juice

- 1 teaspoon of lemon zest

Instructions List:

1. In a saucepan, whisk together milk, heavy cream, sugar, and salt. Heat over medium heat until sugar dissolves and mixture simmers gently around the edges, about 5 minutes. Do not boil.

2. Remove from heat and stir in fresh basil leaves. Let mixture steep for 30 minutes to infuse flavor, then strain through a fine-mesh sieve to remove basil leaves. Discard leaves or reserve for another use.

3. Stir in lemon juice and lemon zest. Let mixture cool completely, at least 2 hours or overnight in the refrigerator.

4. Once chilled, pour the mixture into the Ninja Creami Pint Container.

5. Attach the Creami Paddle to the Ninja Creami Deluxe base unit. Place the container on the base and secure the lid.

6. Select the "Gelato" function and press "Start." The Ninja Creami will automatically churn the gelato for approximately 30 minutes. During churning, a chime will not indicate adding mix-ins for this recipe.

7. After churning is complete, transfer gelato to a container and freeze for at least 4 hours before scooping.

Nutritional Information (per serving, estimated):

- Calories: 480

- Protein: 5g

- Total Fats: 30g
- Fiber: 0g
- Carbohydrates: 45g (includes sugars from milk)

Dark Chocolate Sea Salt Gelato

Time to Prepare: 10 minutes **Ninja Creami Time:** 30 minutes **Servings:** 2

Ingredients:

- 1 1/2 cups of whole milk
- 1 cup of heavy cream
- 3/4 cup granulated sugar
- 1/4 teaspoon of salt
- 6 ounces dark chocolate (60-70% cacao), chopped
- 1 teaspoon of vanilla extract
- Flaky sea salt, for garnish (optional)

Instructions List:

1. In a saucepan, whisk together milk, heavy cream, sugar, and salt. Heat over medium heat until sugar dissolves and mixture simmers gently around the edges, about 5 minutes. Do not boil.
2. Remove from heat and stir in chopped dark chocolate until melted and smooth. Stir in vanilla extract.
3. Let mixture cool completely, at least 2 hours or overnight in the refrigerator.
4. Once chilled, pour the mixture into the Ninja Creami Pint Container.
5. Attach the Creami Paddle to the Ninja Creami Deluxe base unit. Place the container on the base and secure the lid.
6. Select the "Gelato" function and press "Start." The Ninja Creami will automatically churn the gelato for approximately 30 minutes. During churning, a chime will not indicate adding mix-ins for this recipe.
7. After churning is complete, transfer gelato to a container and freeze for at least 4 hours before scooping. Sprinkle with flaky sea salt before serving, if desired.

Nutritional Information (per serving, estimated):

- Calories: 520
- Protein: 5g
- Total Fats: 38g
- Fiber: 0g
- Carbohydrates: 40g (includes sugars from milk)

Mascarpone Berry Gelato

Time to Prepare: 15 minutes **Ninja Creami Time:** 30 minutes **Servings:** 2

Ingredients:

- 1 1/2 cups of whole milk
- 1 cup of heavy cream
- 3/4 cup granulated sugar
- 1/4 teaspoon of salt
- 1/2 cup of mascarpone cheese
- 1 cup of frozen mixed berries

Instructions List:

1. In a saucepan, whisk together milk, heavy cream, sugar, and salt. Heat over medium heat until sugar dissolves and mixture simmers gently around the edges, about 5 minutes. Do not boil.

2. Remove from heat and stir in mascarpone cheese until smooth. Let mixture cool slightly, about 20 minutes.

3. Pour the mixture into a blender and blend until smooth. Strain through a fine-mesh sieve to remove any lumps from the mascarpone cheese. Discard solids or reserve for another use.

4. Stir in frozen mixed berries. Let mixture cool completely, at least 2 hours or overnight in the refrigerator.

5. Once chilled, pour the mixture into the Ninja Creami Pint Container.

6. Attach the Creami Paddle to the Ninja Creami Deluxe base unit. Place the container on the base and secure the lid.

7. Select the "Gelato" function and press "Start." The Ninja Creami will automatically churn the gelato for approximately 30 minutes. During churning, a chime will not indicate adding mix-ins for this recipe.

8. After churning is complete, transfer gelato to a container and freeze for at least 4 hours before scooping.

Nutritional Information (per serving, estimated):

- Calories: 500
- Protein: 7g (from mascarpone cheese)
- Total Fats: 35g (from mascarpone cheese and cream)
- Fiber: 3g (from berries)
- Carbohydrates: 45g (includes sugars from milk and berries)

Pistachio Cardamom Gelato

Time to Prepare: 15 minutes **Ninja Creami Time:** 30 minutes **Servings:** 2

Ingredients:

- 1 1/2 cups of whole milk
- 1 cup of heavy cream
- 3/4 cup granulated sugar
- 1/4 teaspoon of salt

- 1/2 cup of shelled, unsalted pistachios
- 1/2 teaspoon of ground cardamom
- 1 teaspoon of vanilla extract

Instructions List:

1. In a saucepan, whisk together milk, heavy cream, sugar, and salt. Heat over medium heat until sugar dissolves and mixture simmers gently around the edges, about 5 minutes. Do not boil.

2. Remove from heat and stir in ground cardamom. Let mixture steep for 30 minutes to infuse flavor.

3. Strain the mixture through a fine-mesh sieve to remove cardamom particles. Discard solids or reserve for another use.

4. In a food processor, grind the pistachios until finely chopped, but not powdery. Alternatively, you can place the pistachios in a sealed plastic bag and crush them with a rolling pin.

5. Stir the ground pistachios and vanilla extract into the strained milk mixture. Let mixture cool completely, at least 2 hours or overnight in the refrigerator.

6. Once chilled, pour the mixture into the Ninja Creami Pint Container.

7. Attach the Creami Paddle to the Ninja Creami Deluxe base unit. Place the container on the base and secure the lid.

8. Select the "Gelato" function and press "Start." The Ninja Creami will automatically churn the gelato for approximately 30 minutes. During churning, a chime will not indicate adding mix-ins for this recipe.

9. After churning is complete, transfer gelato to a container and freeze for at least 4 hours before scooping.

Nutritional Information (per serving, estimated):

- Calories: 500
- Protein: 5g (from milk)
- Total Fats: 35g (from cream and pistachios)
- Fiber: 2g (from pistachios)
- Carbohydrates: 40g (includes sugars from milk)

Roasted Pear and Gorgonzola Gelato

Time to Prepare: 20 minutes **Ninja Creami Time:** 30 minutes **Servings:** 2

Ingredients:

- 1 pear, ripe but firm (such as Bosc or Bartlett)
- 1 tablespoon of butter
- 2 tablespoons honey
- 1 1/2 cups of whole milk
- 1 cup of heavy cream
- 3/4 cup granulated sugar
- 1/4 teaspoon of salt

- 3 ounces gorgonzola cheese, crumbled

Instructions List:

1. Preheat oven to 400°F (200°C). Line a baking sheet with parchment paper.

2. Peel and core the pear. Cut the pear into 1/2-inch cubes.

3. In a large bowl, toss pear cubes with butter and honey. Spread the pear mixture on the prepared baking sheet.

4. Roast for 15-20 minutes, or until pears are tender and lightly golden brown. Remove from heat and let cool slightly.

5. In a saucepan, whisk together milk, heavy cream, sugar, and salt. Heat over medium heat until sugar dissolves and mixture simmers gently around the edges, about 5 minutes. Do not boil.

6. Remove from heat and stir in crumbled gorgonzola cheese. Let mixture cool completely, at least 2 hours or overnight in the refrigerator.

7. Once chilled, add the roasted pear pieces to the mixture and blend with an immersion blender until smooth. Alternatively, you can transfer the mixture to a blender and blend until smooth. Strain through a fine-mesh sieve to remove any gorgonzola cheese crumbles. Discard solids or reserve for another use.

8. Pour the mixture into the Ninja Creami Pint Container.

9. Attach the Creami Paddle to the Ninja Creami Deluxe base unit. Place the container on the base and secure the lid.

10. Select the "Gelato" function and press "Start." The Ninja Creami will automatically churn the gelato for approximately 30 minutes. During churning, a chime will not indicate adding mix-ins for this recipe.

11. After churning is complete, transfer gelato to a container and freeze for at least 4 hours before scooping.

Nutritional Information (per serving, estimated):

- Calories: 550

- Protein: 8g (from gorgonzola cheese)

- Total Fats: 40g (from gorgonzola cheese, cream, and butter)

- Fiber: 3g (from pear)

- Carbohydrates: 45g (includes sugars from milk, honey, and pear)

Chapter 7: Italian Ice

Classic Lemon Italian Ice

Time to Prepare: 5 minutes **Ninja Creami Time:** 20 minutes (freeze + churn) **Servings:** 2

Ingredients:

- 4 cups of water
- 1 cup of granulated sugar
- 1 cup of freshly squeezed lemon juice (from about 4-5 lemons)
- 1 tablespoon of lemon zest

Instructions List:

1. In a saucepan, whisk together water, sugar, and lemon zest. Heat over medium heat until sugar dissolves and mixture simmers gently, about 5 minutes. Do not boil.

2. Remove from heat and stir in lemon juice. Let mixture cool completely, at least 2 hours or overnight in the refrigerator.

To Freeze:

1. Pour the chilled mixture into the Ninja Creami Pint Container. **Skip the Freeze Step.** Unlike other recipes in this book, this base does not require pre-freezing.

To Make Italian Ice:

2. Attach the Multi-Function Blade to the Ninja Creami Deluxe base unit. Place the container on the base and secure the lid.

3. Select the "Italian Ice" function and press "Start." The Ninja Creami will automatically churn and freeze the Italian ice for approximately 20 minutes. The consistency will be slightly softer than ice cream.

Nutritional Information (per serving, estimated):

- Calories: 100
- Protein: 0g
- Total Fats: 0g
- Fiber: 0g
- Carbohydrates: 25g (from sugar)

Cherry Amaretto Italian Ice

Time to Prepare: 5 minutes **Ninja Creami Time:** 20 minutes (freeze + churn) **Servings:** 2

Ingredients:

- 3 cups of water
- 1 cup of granulated sugar
- 1 cup of pitted, fresh or frozen cherries
- 1/4 cup of amaretto liqueur

Instructions List:

1. In a saucepan, whisk together water and sugar. Heat over medium heat until sugar dissolves and mixture simmers gently, about 5 minutes. Do not boil.

2. Remove from heat and stir in pitted cherries. Let mixture cool slightly, about 10 minutes.

3. Using an immersion blender, blend the cherry mixture until smooth. Alternatively, you can transfer the mixture to a blender and blend until smooth. Strain through a fine-mesh sieve to remove any cherry pits or pulp. Discard solids or reserve for another use.

4. Stir in amaretto liqueur. Let mixture cool completely, at least 2 hours or overnight in the refrigerator.

To Freeze:

1. Pour the chilled mixture into the Ninja Creami Pint Container. **Skip the Freeze Step.** Unlike other recipes in this book, this base does not require pre-freezing.

To Make Italian Ice:

2. Attach the Multi-Function Blade to the Ninja Creami Deluxe base unit. Place the container on the base and secure the lid.

3. Select the "Italian Ice" function and press "Start." The Ninja Creami will automatically churn and freeze the Italian ice for approximately 20 minutes. The consistency will be slightly softer than ice cream.

Nutritional Information (per serving, estimated):

- Calories: 180

- Protein: 0g

- Total Fats: 0g (depending on the amaretto liqueur brand)

- Fiber: 1g (from cherries)

- Carbohydrates: 45g (from sugar and amaretto liqueur)

Pineapple Coconut Italian Ice

Time to Prepare: 5 minutes **Ninja Creami Time:** 20 minutes (freeze + churn) **Servings:** 2

Ingredients:

- 3 cups of water

- 1 cup of granulated sugar

- 1 cup of chopped fresh pineapple

- 1/2 cup of canned coconut milk (light or full-fat)

- 1 teaspoon of lime juice

Instructions List:

1. In a saucepan, whisk together water and sugar. Heat over medium heat until sugar dissolves and mixture simmers gently, about 5 minutes. Do not boil.

2. Remove from heat and stir in chopped fresh pineapple. Let mixture cool slightly, about 10 minutes.

3. Using an immersion blender, blend the pineapple mixture until smooth. Alternatively, you can transfer the mixture to a blender and blend until smooth. Strain through a fine-mesh sieve to remove any pineapple chunks. Discard solids or reserve for another use.

4. Stir in coconut milk and lime juice. Let mixture cool completely, at least 2 hours or overnight in the refrigerator.

To Freeze:

1. Pour the chilled mixture into the Ninja Creami Pint Container. **Skip the Freeze Step.** Unlike other recipes in this book, this base does not require pre-freezing.

To Make Italian Ice:

2. Attach the Multi-Function Blade to the Ninja Creami Deluxe base unit. Place the container on the base and secure the lid.

3. Select the "Italian Ice" function and press "Start." The Ninja Creami will automatically churn and freeze the Italian ice for approximately 20 minutes. The consistency will be slightly softer than ice cream.

Nutritional Information (per serving, estimated):

- Calories: 200

- Protein: 1g (from coconut milk)

- Total Fats: 7g (from coconut milk)

- Fiber: 1g (from pineapple)

- Carbohydrates: 35g (from sugar and lactose in coconut milk)

Watermelon Mint Italian Ice

Time to Prepare: 5 minutes **Ninja Creami Time:** 20 minutes (freeze + churn) **Servings:** 2

Ingredients:

- 3 cups of seedless watermelon, chopped

- 1 cup of water

- 1/2 cup of granulated sugar

- 1/4 cup of fresh mint leaves

Instructions List:

1. In a blender, combine chopped watermelon, water, and sugar. Blend until smooth. Strain through a fine-mesh sieve to remove any watermelon seeds or pulp. Discard solids or reserve for another use.

2. Stir in fresh mint leaves. Let mixture cool completely, at least 2 hours or overnight in the refrigerator.

To Freeze:

1. Pour the chilled mixture into the Ninja Creami Pint Container. **Skip the Freeze Step.** Unlike other recipes in this book, this base does not require pre-freezing.

To Make Italian Ice:

2. Attach the Multi-Function Blade to the Ninja Creami Deluxe base unit. Place the container on the base and secure the lid.

3. Select the "Italian Ice" function and press "Start." The Ninja Creami will automatically churn and freeze the Italian ice for approximately 20 minutes. The consistency will be slightly softer than ice cream.

Nutritional Information (per serving, estimated):

- Calories: 70

- Protein: 0g

- Total Fats: 0g

- Fiber: 1g (from watermelon)

- Carbohydrates: 17g (from sugar)

Blood Orange Italian Ice

Time to Prepare: 5 minutes **Ninja Creami Time:** 20 minutes (freeze + churn) **Servings:** 2

Ingredients:

- 3 cups of water

- 1 cup of granulated sugar

- 1 cup of fresh blood orange juice (from about 3-4 blood oranges)

- 1 tablespoon of blood orange zest

Instructions List:

1. In a saucepan, whisk together water, sugar, and blood orange zest. Heat over medium heat until sugar dissolves and mixture simmers gently, about 5 minutes. Do not boil.

2. Remove from heat and stir in fresh blood orange juice. Let mixture cool completely, at least 2 hours or overnight in the refrigerator.

To Freeze:

1. Pour the chilled mixture into the Ninja Creami Pint Container. **Skip the Freeze Step.** Unlike other recipes in this book, this base does not require pre-freezing.

To Make Italian Ice:

2. Attach the Multi-Function Blade to the Ninja Creami Deluxe base unit. Place the container on the base and secure the lid.

3. Select the "Italian Ice" function and press "Start." The Ninja Creami will automatically churn and freeze the Italian ice for approximately 20 minutes. The consistency will be slightly softer than ice cream.

Nutritional Information (per serving, estimated):

- Calories: 110

- Protein: 0g

- Total Fats: 0g

- Fiber: 1g (from blood oranges)

- Carbohydrates: 27g (from sugar)

Strawberry Basil Italian Ice
Time to Prepare: 5 minutes **Ninja Creami Time:** 20 minutes (freeze + churn) **Servings:** 2

Ingredients:

- 3 cups of water
- 1 cup of granulated sugar
- 1 cup of fresh strawberries, hulled and sliced
- 1/4 cup of fresh basil leaves

Instructions List:

1. In a saucepan, whisk together water and sugar. Heat over medium heat until sugar dissolves and mixture simmers gently, about 5 minutes. Do not boil.

2. Remove from heat and stir in sliced strawberries and fresh basil leaves. Let mixture cool slightly, about 10 minutes.

3. Using an immersion blender, blend the strawberry mixture until smooth. Alternatively, you can transfer the mixture to a blender and blend until smooth. Strain through a fine-mesh sieve to remove any strawberry seeds or basil leaves. Discard solids or reserve for another use.

4. Let mixture cool completely, at least 2 hours or overnight in the refrigerator.

To Freeze:

1. Pour the chilled mixture into the Ninja Creami Pint Container. **Skip the Freeze Step.** Unlike other recipes in this book, this base does not require pre-freezing.

To Make Italian Ice:

2. Attach the Multi-Function Blade to the Ninja Creami Deluxe base unit. Place the container on the base and secure the lid.

3. Select the "Italian Ice" function and press "Start." The Ninja Creami will automatically churn and freeze the Italian ice for approximately 20 minutes. The consistency will be slightly softer than ice cream.

Nutritional Information (per serving, estimated):

- Calories: 120
- Protein: 1g (from strawberries)
- Total Fats: 0g
- Fiber: 2g (from strawberries)
- Carbohydrates: 30g (from sugar)

Mango Lime Italian Ice
Time to Prepare: 5 minutes **Ninja Creami Time:** 20 minutes (freeze + churn) **Servings:** 2

Ingredients:

- 3 cups of water
- 1 cup of granulated sugar
- 1 cup of frozen mango chunks

- 1/4 cup of freshly squeezed lime juice

Instructions List:

1. In a saucepan, whisk together water and sugar. Heat over medium heat until sugar dissolves and mixture simmers gently, about 5 minutes. Do not boil.

2. Remove from heat and stir in frozen mango chunks. Let mixture cool slightly, about 10 minutes.

3. Using an immersion blender, blend the mango mixture until smooth. Alternatively, you can transfer the mixture to a blender and blend until smooth. Strain through a fine-mesh sieve to remove any mango fibers. Discard solids or reserve for another use.

4. Stir in freshly squeezed lime juice. Let mixture cool completely, at least 2 hours or overnight in the refrigerator.

To Freeze:

1. Pour the chilled mixture into the Ninja Creami Pint Container. **Skip the Freeze Step.** Unlike other recipes in this book, this base does not require pre-freezing.

To Make Italian Ice:

2. Attach the Multi-Function Blade to the Ninja Creami Deluxe base unit. Place the container on the base and secure the lid.

3. Select the "Italian Ice" function and press "Start." The Ninja Creami will automatically churn and freeze the Italian ice for approximately 20 minutes. The consistency will be slightly softer than ice cream.

Nutritional Information (per serving, estimated):

- Calories: 150

- Protein: 1g (from mango)

- Total Fats: 0g

- Fiber: 1g (from mango)

- Carbohydrates: 37g (from sugar and mango)

Peach Bellini Italian Ice

Time to Prepare: 5 minutes **Ninja Creami Time:** 20 minutes (freeze + churn) **Servings:** 2

Ingredients:

- 3 cups of water

- 1 cup of granulated sugar

- 1 cup of fresh or frozen peaches, chopped

- 1/4 cup of peach nectar

- 1 tablespoon of champagne or sparkling white wine (optional)

Instructions List:

1. In a saucepan, whisk together water and sugar. Heat over medium heat until sugar dissolves and mixture simmers gently, about 5 minutes. Do not boil.

2. Remove from heat and stir in chopped peaches. Let mixture cool slightly, about 10 minutes.

3. Using an immersion blender, blend the peach mixture until smooth. Alternatively, you can transfer the mixture to a blender and blend until smooth. Strain through a fine-mesh sieve to remove any peach skin or pulp. Discard solids or reserve for another use.

4. Stir in peach nectar and optional champagne or sparkling white wine. Let mixture cool completely, at least 2 hours or overnight in the refrigerator.

To Freeze:

1. Pour the chilled mixture into the Ninja Creami Pint Container. **Skip the Freeze Step.** Unlike other recipes in this book, this base does not require pre-freezing.

To Make Italian Ice:

2. Attach the Multi-Function Blade to the Ninja Creami Deluxe base unit. Place the container on the base and secure the lid.

3. Select the "Italian Ice" function and press "Start." The Ninja Creami will automatically churn and freeze the Italian ice for approximately 20 minutes. The consistency will be slightly softer than ice cream.

Nutritional Information (per serving, estimated):

- Calories: 130 (without champagne)

- Protein: 1g (from peaches)

- Total Fats: 0g (depending on the champagne brand)

- Fiber: 1g (from peaches)

- Carbohydrates: 32g (from sugar and peach nectar)

MEASUREMENT CONVERSION TABLE

Measurement	Imperial (US)	Metric
Volume		
1 teaspoon	1 tsp	5 milliliters
1 tablespoon	1 tbsp	15 milliliters
1 fluid ounce	1 fl oz	30 milliliters
1 cup	1 cup	240 milliliters
1 pint	1 pt	473 milliliters
1 quart	1 qt	0.95 liters
1 gallon	1 gal	3.8 liters
Weight		
1 ounce	1 oz	28 grams
1 pound	1 lb	454 grams
Temperature		
32°F	32°F	0°C
212°F	212°F	100°C
Other		
1 stick of butter	1 stick	113 grams

CONCLUSION

Congratulations on completing your Ninja Creami Deluxe adventure! You now have a collection of vibrant flavors and textures to create refreshing treats that will delight everyone. This journey was not only about the delicious results, but also about the fun and creativity of the process. Each step, from blending fresh fruits to swirling in decadent sauces, allows you to personalize your frozen treats. Remember, these recipes are just a starting point. Feel free to experiment with different ingredients and flavor combinations to create your own unique creations. So gather your favorite fruits, explore the aisles of your grocery store, and let your inner dessert scientist shine! With the Ninja Creami Deluxe at your disposal, the possibilities for frozen delights are limitless. Enjoy!

RECIPES INDEX

Strawberry Balsamic Sorbet 51

Strawberry Basil Italian Ice 66

Thai Tea Ice Cream 10

Toasted Coconut Almond Ice Cream 14

Toasted Marshmallow and Graham Cracker Crumble 18

Watermelon Basil Sorbet 50

Watermelon Mint Italian Ice 64

White Chocolate Chips and Cranberry Sauce 23

Made in the USA
Coppell, TX
26 June 2024